the epicurean collector

Patrick Dunne

with the Editors of
Southern Accents

Photographs by
Charles E. Walton IV

the epicurean collector

exploring the world of culinary antiques

A Bulfinch Press Book   Little, Brown and Company   Boston New York London

For my father, who celebrated food, and my mother, who civilized it.

Additional illustration credits on page 177.

First edition

Library of Congress Cataloging-in-Publication Data
Dunne, Patrick.
    The epicurean collector / Patrick Dunne, with the editors of
    Southern Accents—1st ed.
      p. cm.
    Includes index.
    ISBN 0-8212-2759-9
      1. Kitchen utensils—Collectibles. 2. Kitchen utensils—History.
      I. Southern accents. II. Title.
TX656.D86 2002

2001043664

Designed by Jean Wilcox
Bulfinch Press is an imprint and trademark of Little, Brown and Company (Inc.)
Printed in Singapore

contents

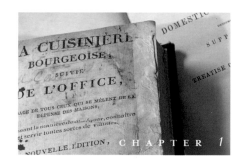

  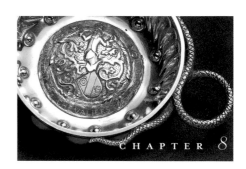

CHAPTER 9

CHAPTER 10

acknowledgments

Gratitude is a small word to express what I feel for the kindnesses of: Charles Mackie, whose book this also is. He encouraged me to begin writing on the subject, had the originality to steer me toward the right areas, and was my coauthor on many early essays; Charles Walton, whose brilliant photographs and joie de vivre have made me look at things quite differently; the many editors at *Southern Accents*, especially Frances MacDougall, for their belief that this book should happen and forbearance toward my eccentricities; Kerry Moody, whose styling, style, and good sense are seen in these pages; Jan Longone and her Food and Wine Library, both precious American resources; Michele Bray, for help in research and tireless rereading and criticisms; and Denise Buford, for all the work behind the scenes. Finally, Zoubir Tabout, for all the real and imagined tisanes that sustained me.

introduction

Like conversation at late-night suppers in New Orleans, the content of these pages has been kept deliberately light. Serious food scholars may be disappointed, but others, I hope, will be diverted as they savor the odd and the familiar in new settings. The field of culinary history is fresh and much primary material awaits researchers. Like all history, the story of how we eat is really just another part of the long tale about being human, one necessarily full of vast complications and contradictions. It may be truly coherent only within an individual lifespan or at best that of a particular tribe.

Brillat-Savarin, that enormously fat and enormously witty French philosopher of food, boasted in the early nineteenth century *"Dis-moi ce que tu manges, je te dirai qui tu es."* It may have been true when he was writing *The Physiology of Taste* that he could tell what you were by knowing what you ate, but now such a conclusion begs for deeper analysis.

Among other things, we want to know how food was enjoyed, the implications and cultural context of its discovery and development, and from a collector's point of view, the implements that were uniquely created for use in serving and satisfying new appetites. The great culinary changes that began at the end of the seventeenth century not only set new standards for food preparation but transformed the styles of its presentation and produced an incredible outpouring of craftsmanship.

These essays, which appeared over a period of five years in *Southern Accents* magazine, are not intended to tell the whole story; rather, they are hearthside gossip meant to arouse reveries — like an aroma, suggestive but insubstantial. They may seem quirky, opinionated, and shamelessly Eurocentric, as I am. The next tier of study will certainly make accessible comparative cultural research using Asian, African, and especially the profoundly rich Islamic sources to enhance our understanding of foodways. When these are sifted through, much will be rewritten. Rome was as syncretistic as America is today. Gustatory tastes do not collapse with empires; they alter with availability of ingredients, the whimsy of fashion, and the confidence of cooks. The palate is our most conservative instrument; its judgments and desires change only reluctantly and slowly. What classical civilization left behind in the various bread bowls of barbarian Europe became the leaven of culinary developments for nearly two millennia.

The chief theme of this book is the decorative effects on table style during the last three centuries that resulted from the discovery of new foods and new techniques and the reinterpretation of old ones.

Certainly the way we have managed ourselves at table reveals the pattern not only of our appetites but of our aesthetic tastes and social organization. The accumulation of proper culinary equipment and the corresponding etiquette it requires have long been a means of identifying, excluding, controlling, and, yes, it must be said, sometimes even civilizing unruly humans. During the last two hundred years, the household meal was very much the principal familial ritual in the cult of domesticity. Sons learned hierarchy and paternal tyranny at the table, daughters daintiness and the shrewdly submissive maneuver. In most houses the dining table symbolically became both the magic and madness that bound families together. It was the tribunal where serious decisions were taken and the place that made and broke rebellious children, casual guests, and careless social climbers. Its artifacts and customs were crucible and schoolroom. Knowledge of its refinements and familiarity with its elaborate and evolving vocabulary were important to almost everybody.

This predominance of the table has largely disappeared in all but the most traditional enclaves, and along with it many of its finely wrought trappings. Today many people eat hurriedly and horridly, en route to geographical or electronic destinations that have changed the rhythms of life. Today's eating implements are as disposable and elemental as those of cavemen. Traditional formal meals, once the focal point of social concourse, are disintegrating in the gravitational pull of a new culture. Also for the first time in Western civilization — indeed, in human history — the gathering, preparing, and consuming of food is not the chief daily preoccupation of most people. The plethora of new cookbooks published every year belies our estrangement from the kitchen and will bewilder the next millennium. It will seem that all we did was stir pots — and what pots! — filled with ingredients borrowed from every corner of the earth. Never has so much sustenance been available so instantaneously, nor has satisfaction been more elusive. Certainly the nostalgia for food in all its nurturing aspects has never been so strong. This book is part of that nostalgia and a protest that savoring style should still be an essential part of the daily human banquet.

looking for *f*ormulas, cooking by a *b*ook

From time to time there is a measurable quickening in human affairs — moments when quite suddenly, seemingly out of nowhere, some half-forgotten ideas appear fresh or a boundless sense of confidence expresses itself in original ways. Out of this something noticeably distinct emerges. For reasons not completely comprehensible, during the second half of the seventeenth century things began to change in the kitchens of Europe, and the epicenter of these changes was France. The word *revolution* has become trivialized today, but a revolution is really what it was.

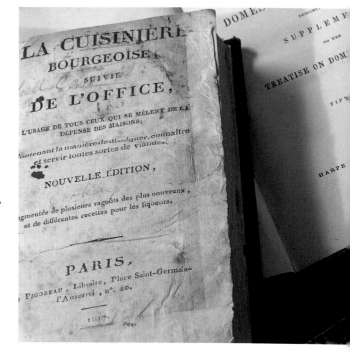

Many nineteenth-century cookbooks, such as Things a Lady Would Like to Know *(1880), were as much manuals instructing women on how to complete daily chores as collections of recipes. Recipes often circulated in manuscript form as well, and handwritten cookbooks were treasured items.*

A notebook kept by a nineteenth-century Alabama woman incorporated clippings and handwritten notes.

Perhaps the most influential book to come out of the French culinary revolution was La Cuisinière bourgeoise *(left), first published in 1746. New editions were issued periodically; the book pictured is an edition from 1817. Catharine E. Beecher, who wrote the* Domestic Receipt-Book *(right) in 1846, saw domestic education as an important element in the crusade for women's advancement.*

The culinary revolution, which transformed not just the types of food consumed but its preparation and presentation, was part of the epoch's general mood of agitated inquiry. A connection, still largely unexplored, existed between changes in the kitchen and the simultaneous intellectual ferment of the age. Coincidence alone cannot explain the number of personalities identified with great discoveries in the new sciences who also had an uncommon interest in food. Samuel Pepys, the great English diarist and friend of nearly every important experimenter, was as fascinated by the accomplishments of a good chef as by the electrifying theories of Isaac Newton.

Observing, recording, and repeating experiments may have opened new dimensions in astronomy, physics, and chemistry, but this methodology was already well established around the stoves of Europe. It is hard to imagine refined cuisine without the ability to calculate time or determine quantity. Yet before 1600, clocks were not terribly accurate, and the precise measurement of time was one of the greatest challenges for the period's budding scientists. A clock quickly became one of the essential furnishings of the new kitchen, as did scales. It was in the seventeenth century that the French mathematician Gilles Personne de Roberval ensured the precise measurement of foods by improving the old Roman balance which had depended on a string and fulcrum. Accurate measurement of time, heat, and volume was as crucial to the production of a good cake as to the prediction of the movement of heavenly bodies.

A "modern" cuisine, incorporating these new scientific principles, began to find fluent expression in the growing body of published treatises on cooking. We have truly been people of the book. Not only have our ethics and our morals been shaped by the scriptures of monotheism, but so have our menus. While the Pentateuch and the Koran have much to say about food preparation, there is another sense in which that concept is true. Secular cookery texts have propounded secrets that have been changing palates since the invention of writing. For two thousand years, but most especially during the last three hundred, kitchens of the West have been deluged by books containing recipes, household hints, and remedies. Their influence is incalculable.

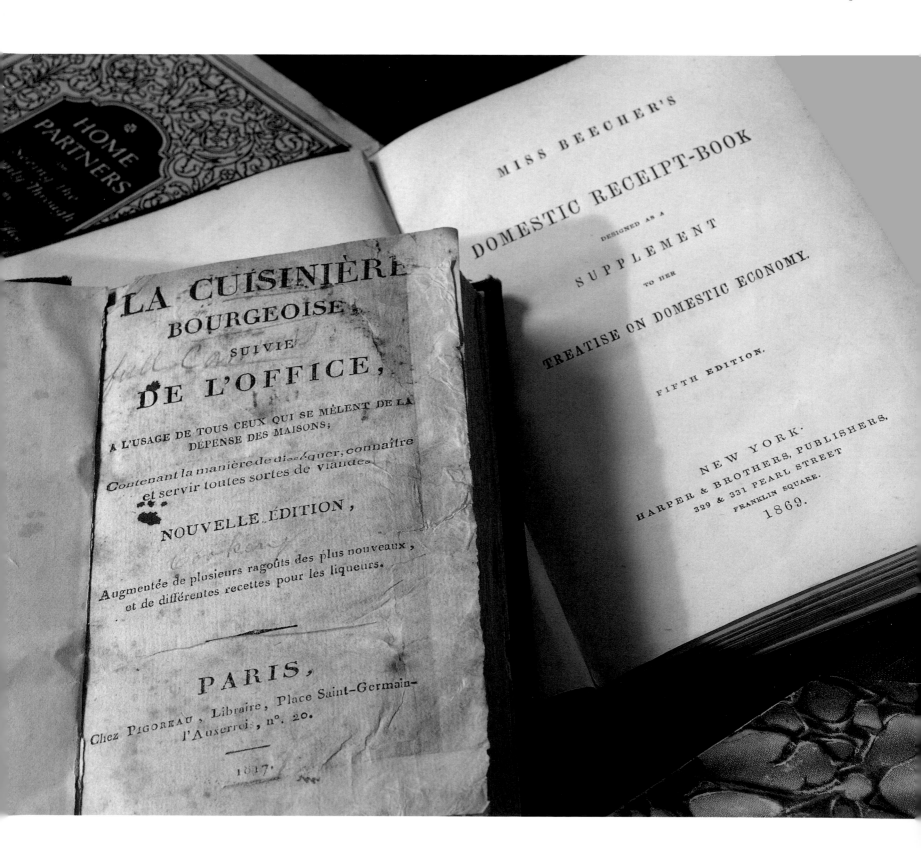

Alexis Soyer, author of Soyer's Cookery Book, *first published in London in 1854 as* A Shilling Cookery for the People, Embracing an Entirely New System of Plain Cookery and Domestic Economy, *translated the French culinary gospel for ordinary English households in the mid-nineteenth-century.*

But for a long time people learned to cook or taught others to cook without written manuals. Indeed, so strong was the oral tradition in kitchen arts that reading early cookbooks today leaves the impression that preparing anything from their sketchy outlines would be nearly impossible.

Until the late eighteenth century, detailed instructions for cooking were rarely written down. It was assumed every cook would know enough to complete a recipe. Whereas Chinese cuisine has rested on a well-established body of printed literature for four thou-

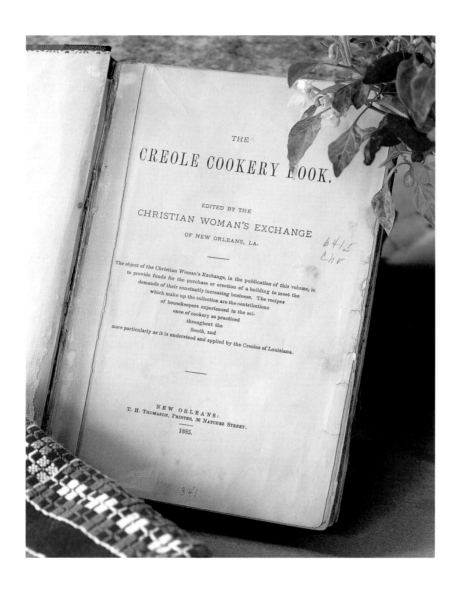

sand years, the oldest Western cookbook surviving more or less intact is the one ascribed to Apicius, a Roman gourmand born about 25 B.C. He reputedly committed suicide when his fortune became insufficient to satisfy his prodigious appetites. The book is actually a compilation of recipes from various sources in antiquity, including a number from ancient Greece. It may have been assembled long after his death, as the oldest surviving manuscript form of this book, sometimes called *Ars Magirica* (The Art of the Cook), is from the eighth

Until quite late, cooks in New Orleans followed French manuals or handed-down recipes and manuscripts. The first "native" cookbooks appeared almost simultaneously in the 1880s. The Creole Cookery Book was published in 1885 and marked the beginning of a fascination with indigenous cuisine.

The Compleat Housewife, *by Eliza Smith, published by William Parks in Williamsburg, Virginia in 1742, was the first cookbook to be printed in America. Although many recipes were of English origin, the book remained popular into the early nineteenth century.*

Good cooking and good housekeeping were often presented as being connected to morality and virtue. Many early cookbooks were as much guides to the principled life as collections of recipes.

century. It was first printed about 1420 in Venice under the title *De re coquinaria, libri deces* (Ten Books on Cooking), or more simply, *De re culinaria*. Whatever its origin, it gives us an invaluable insight into the culinary tastes of the ancient world.

Thousands of cookbooks were written over the next two millennia. Some were poetical, celebrating great meals or dishes without attempting to give any clue about their preparation. This genre traces its lineage from the Greeks through Rabelais and Grimod de la Reynière and into the "modern" era. Other food writers took a theological or moral approach, seeking to tie right living to divinely inspired menus. Medical food writing was simply a secularization of this impulse, exhorting readers to eat or to avoid certain foods for reasons of health, potency, or long life. This approach was often taken up by apologists with commercial agendas whose aim was to promote foods so rare and costly that they needed some justification. Some cookbooks were primarily accounts of royal or noble feasts, and are valuable for the menus they disclose. Later this kind of writing was democratized and became blueprints for more humble entertaining, and often included lectures on etiquette.

Finally, there were books, few at first, that actually sought to be instructive. Usually written by professionals for professionals, they eventually discovered the broader audience of eager yet ignorant householders. The first French cookbook of this type, *Le Viandier*, was written by Guillaume Tirel, called Taillevent, around 1375 for the royal cooks of Charles V. It gives nearly twenty sauce recipes and detailed instructions on how to prepare ragouts. A great success, it was reprinted for several centuries.

Serious cookbook writing began to emerge tentatively in the fifteenth century but came fully into its own only in the eighteenth century, largely due to two factors: inexpensive printing and a larger number of cooks who could read. Over the years, cookbooks both recorded the development of new cuisines and actually helped invent them. They are invaluable not just for noting what and how people were eating but for providing social history as well. Until recently, culinary fashions reflected the realities of political power. In the sixteenth century, Italian cookbooks dominated; in the early seventeenth century, Spanish books were influential, and by the end of the seventeenth century French chefs wielded more power than the Sun King himself.

Although earlier manuscripts exist, the first cookbook printed in English was Richard Pynson's *Boke of Cookery* in 1500. No matter that he was French, from Normandy, for then as now, kitchen news traveled fast. During the ensuing five hundred years there was such a continual exchange of information that plagiarism became a completely acceptable practice for cookbook writers.

The earliest known cookbook to have been printed in America was Eliza Smith's *The Compleat Housewife* (1742), but it was essentially identical to her earlier English book. Most eighteenth-century American cooks relied heavily on English publishers or handwritten manuscripts. It is telling that the most valuable bequest Martha Washington made was her own handwritten kitchen notes, left to her granddaughter Nelly Custis Lewis. It wasn't until 1796 that the first authentically American cookbook, Amelia Simmons's *American Cookery*, appeared. Although a debt to English sources was apparent, it nevertheless included some indigenous recipes for pumpkin pie and watermelon-rind pickles. It retained its preeminence for nearly fifty years. The first truly Southern cookbook, *The Virginia Housewife* (1824), was the work of Mary Randolph, who was greatly influenced by the French culinary tradition. Her collection included dishes typical of the South, such as turnip greens, catfish, and okra soup.

Post–Civil War America saw an avalanche of books, magazines, and manuals aimed at teaching women how to manage households, set tables, and save labor. Practically every county and town produced cookbooks that featured local variations of recipes. Collecting these today preserves a footprint of the evolution of cuisine and an insight into the strenuous realities of household management in the nineteenth century. They also furnish an invaluable lexicon of forgotten dishes, whose names endure but whose ingredients are forgotten. Often tattered, sometimes handsome and well illustrated, these cookbooks are a testament to humanity's enduring desire not merely to survive but to take creative delight in nourishment.

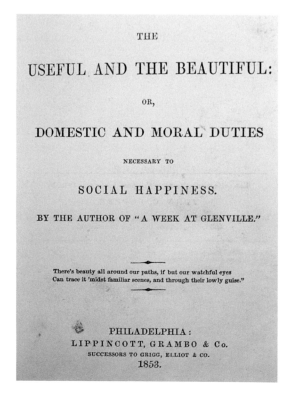

THE

USEFUL AND THE BEAUTIFUL:

OR,

DOMESTIC AND MORAL DUTIES

NECESSARY TO

SOCIAL HAPPINESS.

BY THE AUTHOR OF "A WEEK AT GLENVILLE."

There's beauty all around our paths, if but our watchful eyes
Can trace it 'midst familiar scenes, and through their lowly guise."

PHILADELPHIA:
LIPPINCOTT, GRAMBO & Co.
SUCCESSORS TO GRIGG, ELLIOT & CO.
1853.

CHAPTER 2

tending the fires

Between the domestication of fire and the introduction of the cast-iron stove in the nineteenth century, kitchen technology saw little fundamental innovation. The hearth of a Roman matron would have been familiar to an early Mississippi Valley housewife, but the microwave oven would have confounded Lewis and Clark more than a banquet with Odysseus. Epochs are separated by more than time.

Gallier House's cast-iron stove was a major departure from hearth cooking, but smoke was still a major inconvenience, as well as temperature regulation.

Cooking over the open flame is gratifying but also difficult and limiting. While various contraptions allowed for some stewing and frying over a fire, hearth cooking was not well suited to the preparation of the complicated new sauces and dishes that were beginning to find their way into professionally supervised aristocratic kitchens. The introduction of masonry stoves, called *potagers,* into privileged French households toward the end of the seventeenth century began to solve this problem. The tops of these *potagers* were divided into small chambers that held charcoal and acted as burners. These "stew holes," as the English sometimes called them, could be replenished with coals periodically during the cooking process. The heat of these chambers was easier to control and allowed for simmering.

Although it appeared to be a modern invention at the time, *potager*-type appliances had been known throughout the Mediterranean lands at the end of the Renaissance. They were also used in the ancient world, because something very similar was discovered in the House of the Stags during the excavations at Herculaneum, an ancient Italian city buried in the eruption of Vesuvius in A.D. 79. By the end of the seventeenth century, masonry stoves had become common enough to be included in A. C. d'Aviler's treatise on architecture, *Explication de termes d'architecture* (Paris, 1691). A rare example of an American *potager* still in operation can be found at the Hermann-Grima House in New Orleans. It was installed when the house was built in 1831.

The inefficiency of hearth cooking caught the attention of Count Rumford, born Benjamin Thompson near Boston in 1753. "The loss of heat and the waste of fuel in these kitchens is altogether incredible," he declared, and in 1795 set about designing an iron stove that would both contain and conserve heat and vent the smoke through an enclosed flue. It is somewhat paradoxical that Rumford should have led a major skirmish in the kitchen revolution. An avowed anti-revolutionary in a time of great political change, he was nearly convicted of treason after the American War of Independence for his sympathy to the crown.

His experiments with the stove caught the fancy of a new patron, Prince Maximilian, the future king of Bavaria, who gave him

Built around 1831, the potager in New Orleans's historic Herman Grima house is fitted with small chambers that held charcoal to heat the stove top.

Below left: *Hearth cooking continued to be a preferred method of food preparation for centuries, but the soot, the smoke, and the unpredictability of the fire made it something of a headache.*

Below right: *It may be rudimentary in its function, but the beauty of the nineteenth-century tile stove presages the current obsession with beautiful cooking appliances.*

a title for his efforts. Similar cooking stoves existed in the Han Dynasty (202 B.C.–220 A.D.) in China. Literary descriptions give this stove a chimney, a platform in front of the fire chamber, and five cooking holes, making it a close cousin to the invention that was to transform Western cooking a millennium later.

Iron stoves had already been manufactured in colonial America by the Saugus Blast Furnace Company. First produced around 1650, the Saugus stove was basically no more than an iron box that could be heated. By the late eighteenth century several manufactories in Pennsylvania were producing variants, and the first satisfactory iron cookstove, known as the Baltimore Cook Stove, was marketed by William T. James in Troy, New York, in 1815. Essentially these were "stewing" stoves. Baking and roasting were still done in brick ovens. Even England's modern-minded Prince Regent, Francophile in so many matters *culinaire*, still preferred meat to be done to a turn upon a spit.

By the 1860s there were dozens of manufactories in the United States producing cookstoves, the grandest and most in demand being Mr. Currier's "Kitchen Queen." In the decades immediately after the Civil War, only the most reactionary cooks resisted this new mode of cooking, and most cookbook writers assumed that if a housekeeper could choose, an iron stove would be used.

Opinion, however, was not always unanimously favorable. Early cast-iron stoves had the inconvenient habit of cracking from the heat and flooding the kitchen with yet more smoke. Also, the utensils inherited or accumulated by the householder were virtually useless on these stoves. Catharine Beecher, of the famous and formidable nineteenth-century American family of moral watchdogs, complained of the smell of iron stoves. Her sister took a loftier tone. "An open fireplace is an altar of patriotism," Harriet Beecher Stowe declared. "Would our Revolutionary fathers have gone barefooted and bleeding over the snows to defend air-tight stoves and cooking ranges?"

Perhaps not, but certainly subsequent generations of cooks might have done so, despite the awesome efforts required to keep such stoves in order. The work needed to maintain a cast-iron stove was much greater than that required for an open hearth. Coal was preferred to wood as fuel, because much less of it was required to produce fierce heat, but the poor ventilation of these stoves and kitchens in general was a problem. The unhealthy level of carbon monoxide in the kitchen remained a menace to the cook.

In 1849, James Young of Scotland discovered a coal-refining process that produced a cleaner-burning fuel oil. Then in 1858 oil was discovered in the United States, ushering in an age of kerosene.

The introduction of gas and electricity as heat sources for cast-iron stoves radically transformed cooking habits all over the world. Waverley Root and Richard de Rochemont, in *Eating in America* (1976), summed up the diehard judgment on the change. "Dare we suggest," they write in magisterial tones reminiscent of the Beechers, "that the modern stove, superb though it is as a labor-saving device, makes it possible for almost anyone to cook acceptably, but almost impossible for anyone to cook divinely."

CHAPTER *3*

ironing things *out*

Despite these fancy innovations, until the early twentieth century much serious cooking in most households continued to be done on an open hearth or on small portable braziers. To accomplish this type of cooking, an enormous variety of iron tools and gadgets were required. Always utilitarian and often fancifully detailed, they express man's eternal ingenuity in solving everyday problems.

Delicate waffles and wafers were produced in monstrously heavy irons. The engraved patterns appeared on the waffle in relief in designs to suit every cook's whim, from hearts to family coats of arms.

The gods of Olympus had the good sense to create their own immortal blacksmith, Hephaestus. Despite his limping gait, he was married to the beautiful Aphrodite. Strong craftsmanship was thus allied to beauty. This makes it easier to conceive of a craft that delivers from anvil and brute muscle objects often delicate, refined, even playful.

The Iron Age is said to have begun about 1000 B.C. The metal appears in nature quite plentifully, and humans learned to fabricate from it small objects like beads and rings. Blacksmiths and forges were common in the classical world, and they produced household articles of considerable sophistication. Substantial evidence of their work survives. Much Roman food was cooked on iron braziers or in iron cauldrons over open fires. The nearly complete kitchen preserved beneath volcanic ash and excavated at Herculaneum gives us a sense of the iron pots used in antiquity. These simple cooking vessels may have incidentally provided a much-needed dietary supplement as well. When certain acidic foods are cooked in iron pots, the infused iron content can be increased dramatically.

By the late Middle Ages, ironworking had reached such a highly developed state that it was subdivided into several trades: cutlers who made knife blades, farm implements, and swords; armorers; nailers; locksmiths; and blacksmiths, who made decorative ironwork and utilitarian domestic objects.

The blacksmith was a technician crucial to cooks, especially wherever the "wide fire," or hearth, remained the chief means of cooking. The kitchen was a hazardous workplace. Burns suffered while performing hearth tasks were one of the major causes of female deaths before the middle of the nineteenth century. A battery of sturdy and well-balanced cooking equipment was therefore extremely important in even the simplest cottage.

The pothook, or *crémaillère,* as it was called in France, was a ratchetted affair which hung in the fireplace and had a wide hook on one end to hold the handle of a pot or kettle. Being adjustable, it provided some regulation of heat. So essential was this piece of equipment that to throw a housewarming party in France is to *pendre la crémaillère* ("hang the pothook"). Cooks also required trivets, three-legged stands that rested over or near the fire to support pots and

Before the nineteenth century, sugar was available only in hard cones and had to be cut with specially constructed nippers. Although some nippers were handheld, others were mounted in special boxes like this one to prevent the escape of even the tiniest pieces. Sugar was such a valuable ingredient that it was kept under lock and key.

The eighteenth-century penchant for mechanical contraptions extended to kitchen conveniences, including such wizardry as this iron tournebroche, *or rotatable spit, circa 1770.*

With the convenience of adjustable pothooks, or crémaillères, the same fire could provide everything from a raging boil to a gentle simmer.

These French andirons transcended the functional with their graceful designs.

Artfully designed hooks, such as this eighteenth-century French râtelier de cuisine (kitchen rack),
could be placed around the kitchen and moved as needed. From left to right are a long-handled skim-
mer and three salamanders (browning utensils), all of eighteenth-century hand-wrought iron.

Like the mythic salamander that lived in the fire, kitchen salamanders lived in the cooking embers.
The white-hot implement was held over casseroles and other dishes to brown the tops. The browning
element of today's ovens is still known as a salamander. These two examples date to circa 1780.

20

A set of decorative hanging hooks, or couronne d'office, *kept food within ready reach of the cook.*

kettles. Cranes, or *servantes,* fitted with swinging arms from which large cooking pots hung operated in hearths, allowing the cook to temporarily pull a bubbling pot out of the fireplace without the effort and danger involved in unhooking it. Many cranes were of the simplest design, but their valued status can be inferred by the highly decorative, even exuberant, examples surviving from prosperous households. The long handles of frying pans were sometimes fashioned into swan necks. The feet on toasters or the handles on large spoons or cooking forks were pulled and twisted into curlicues as if they were molasses. Painters such as Jean-Baptiste-Siméon Chardin and Jean-Baptiste Lallemand have left us canvases that are an enduring record of how these useful objects decorated the ample hearth rooms of eighteenth-century houses.

Some traditional ironwork designs can be identified with a specific locality, such as the heart shape, which is frequently found in French and Scottish as well as some early Dutch-American work. However, most decorative motifs were found throughout Western Europe and America and reflected both the possibilities and limitations imposed by the material itself. The scroll was an obvious way to finish the end of a piece of metal. The ram's-head shape may have come from the ancient world. "Twisting" and "upsetting," which is a blobbing at the end of an implement to make an orb or mushroom-like finial, was as logical as it was aesthetic and occurred quite naturally to blacksmiths everywhere. Because metalwork is by nature very linear, there was less of an impulse to respond to changing fashions as the other decorative arts did. Styles tended to endure much longer. For this reason it is difficult to date iron objects solely on a stylistic basis.

Making kitchen utensils was often a cottage industry: sometimes whole families were involved. Although men dominated the craft, women occasionally worked iron as well. Because they were employed to make equipment to meet special needs or fit into special places, blacksmiths were innovators and problem solvers, the self-taught engineers of the day.

the *collision* with condiments

The dynamic synergy between new ingredients and new cooking methods sparked culinary experimentation, changed eating habits, and spurred the embellishment of the table throughout the ages. Great transformations are often set in motion by the merest grain of novelty, and so it was in feudal Europe. The metamorphosis began by the whetting of rather drab early medieval appetites with pinches of sugar, salt, and spice.

The high price of spices meant consumers kept them locked away in boxes, like these early-nineteenth-century English painted tole safes.

salt

No condiment has been so celebrated or surrounded with ceremony as salt. It has made a triumphal procession across the tables of the past in "cellars" ranging from humble to ornate. That it has practically disappeared along with sugar from public display makes one question the taste if not the sense of our age.

Since it is a food that also forms an essential chemical composition in the body, our culinary relationship to salt has been uniquely biological. Plato included it in a short list of acceptable foods for his Republic, and the classical writer Plutarch described it as the "noblest of nourishment."

How the ancient Romans presented it on their tables is unclear, but if the book of recipes collected by Apicius from the first century A.D. is any indication, their food was loaded with it. The city of Rome itself grew as a Tiber port on the Via salaria, or Salt Road. Its soldiers were once paid in part with salt, and when coin was substituted, it came to be called *salary*. Indeed, so greedy were the Romans for first-quality salt that they were drawn to Palestine and the Dead Sea as a source, changing both political and religious history.

Curiously, salt, which is found worldwide, was once considered a precious commodity. While it was always regarded as an emblem of a host's hospitality, its use was encrusted with superstition and ritual. Traditionally it was interpreted as a sign of amity; the ancient Roman orator Cicero cited the already ancient proverb "you must eat many measures of salt" together before you can be good friends with someone. A gift of salt brought good fortune; spilling it courted disaster.

Like all luxuries, salt could be dangerous: it was sometimes used to conceal lethal poisons such as arsenic. For this reason, by the end of the Middle Ages it was locked into fantastic-looking objects made of precious metals and jewels called nefs or navettes, so called because they were often shaped like sailing ships or castle towers. Anyone looking at the navette made by the master craftsman Pierre le Flamand around 1528, with its ship of mother of pearl, prow of gold and silver, and golden sails at full mast now in the Victoria and Albert Museum of London, can only marvel at the joy taken in this condiment. Owning such a saltcellar was considered a privilege for a

Craftsmen often lavished their energy on miniature objects such as these silver and turquoise saltcellars from the Arts and Crafts movement (1870–1900).

The high drama of Napoleonic France required equally appropriate table accoutrements. Because blue or clear glass liners helped forestall the corrosive effects of salt, housekeepers could be liberated from the drudgery of cleaning this nineteenth-century French saltcellar.

A careless servant or some guest's larcenous deed left a wealthy English family short one sterling saltcellar. The rococo-style example in the background is an 1829 copy of Robert Hennell's 1773 original (foreground).

Archaeological references provided revival designs in silver and glass. These miniature copies, circa 1913, of ancient Roman bowls were the last stand for the master saltcellar. Following World War I, individual saltcellars and tiny spoons littered the well-appointed table.

king or prince, and the inventories of royal households indicate just how valuable they were. Louis I of Anjou had twenty-one jeweled *salières,* or saltcellars, and Charles V had seventy-seven.

By the Renaissance, great artists were called in to decorate the table with grand saltcellars. The most famous is the one created in gold for Francis I of France by Benvenuto Cellini. Few creations were as extravagant as the saltcellar created by an unknown Italian master that is now in the Prado museum in Madrid. A bowl of onyx edged in gold and rimmed with rubies and enamel is supported by a gold figure of a mermaid, her elegant curving tail set with rubies and emeralds reaching a rocky base of gold and enamel.

As late as 1650, writers on etiquette were advising diners not to dip their food directly into the communal saltcellar but to use the tips of their knives and to be careful not to spill any on the table. The reg-

ularity with which this advice was given indicates it went largely unheeded.

Individual saltcellars began to emerge in the seventeenth century, and with the development of distinct place settings they became an indispensable part of gracious dining. Another utensil, the pierced caster, or shaker, which seems to have been a French invention, appeared around this time as well. Most often used for sugar or pepper, it occasionally held salt. Some early American examples in silver survive, but a shaker was poorly adapted to the coarse and hydrous salt of this period. Peter Kalm, a Swedish botanist who visited America in the late eighteenth century, remarked that most salt in the English colonies came from the West Indies and that it was particularly "corrosive," which may explain a marked predominance of glass and ceramic saltcellars on American tables.

The monumental size of these Royal Worcester porcelain saltcellars exquisitely flaunted their owner's affluence. The ivory spoon is French.

This pair of 1870 sterling silver saltcellars by Gorham was a delightful present for a twenty-fifth wedding anniversary.

A French etiquette book of the eighteenth century insisted a well-set table have saltcellars *"à portée de main des convives"* — that is, "within the reach of each guest." For any collector wondering at the great number and variety of antique saltcellars, this may provide an answer. The manual *Robert's Guide for Butlers and Other Household Staff* (1827), written by a former slave who had gone north to Boston, instructed servants to "put out your salts, which should be six in number as this is the regular quantity for ten to dinner."

The earliest form was the "trencher," a square or polygonal box, sometimes but rarely lidded and occasionally divided to accommodate a second condiment. This simple and useful form, with its solid appearance, gave way to the fanciful *rocaille* shapes popular during the Louis XV period (1715–74): shell and botanical forms, which in a way prefigure the Art Nouveau styles of the 1900s.

The most popular shape was the "cauldron," a round or oval bowl supported on several legs. It made its debut in the eighteenth century, endured through the nineteenth, and was revived in the early twentieth with the renewed taste for Georgian design. The neoclassical cellars that were introduced at the end of the eighteenth century, great favorites during the Regency in England and the early American republic, were a vase shape, usually with a pedestal foot, and often with a liner of blue or clear glass.

Saltcellars charm the subtle collector because craftsmen lavished their full decorative energy on these miniature objects, the restrictions imposed by their size making their creative expression all the more fascinating.

Queens usually know how to pack for trips, especially if they intend to dazzle the public. When Sheba's sovereign rode into Judea, her camels were loaded with veils, buckets of jewels, and some gold for bribes. But the real treasure was nearly a ton of spices she had hauled along to satisfy a king. Her fortune rested on the spice trade, and she was determined to keep the greedy Solomon from going too far with his idea for building a spice-hunting navy. Sheba (now known as Yemen) was ideally positioned on the edge of the Arabian Peninsula, facing India's Malabar Coast, whence most spices were shipped.

For thousands of years a strategy of controlling the supply of spices served "oriental" potentates well — that is, until the fifteenth century, when a spice-crazed Europe launched aggressive explorers with modern weaponry to break the monopoly that had kept sultans rich and prices astronomically high. Seafaring exploration might have happened anyway, but these exploits were hastened on by avaricious merchants hoping to cut out a middleman. Spices created so much wealth for the Italian city-states that in a sense they could be said to have paid for the Renaissance. For a few hundred years it was recipes, not religion, that formulated foreign policy.

The bouquet of rare spices that tantalized palates and emptied purses remained fairly constant for what seemed an eternity. It included cinnamon, pepper, cardamom, ginger, mustard, nutmeg, and cloves. Neolithic peoples in the Indus plain lived in one of the world's earliest spice-trading centers more than four thousand years ago: Archaeologists have found remnants of turmeric, ginger, and mustard as well as evidence of spice-grinding stones in Rehman Dehri. A thousand years later, Egyptian papyri begin recording the sophisticated tastes of early Egyptians. They used most of the non-American spices known to us today for culinary flavorings and for elaborate embalming and funerary rites.

Neither, it seemed, was the Divine impervious to the enchantments of these tasty condiments. They were regularly used in sacrifice and amulets. When God instructed Moses on the ingredients of a sacred oil used for anointing kings and priests, cinnamon and cassia, a stronger type of cinnamon from China, were included.

Apocalyptic scriptures left no doubt how crucial spice could be, for the disappearance of cinnamon was among the terrible signs heralding the world's end.

Black pepper, the fruit of the *Piper nigrum* plant, held pride of place as the most popular spice in the West. A native of India, it was first mentioned in Sanskrit documents more than three thousand years ago. Alexander the Great plundered pepper stores along his path of conquest, and Emperor Marcus Aurelius realized that the Roman demand for pepper was so great, not taxing it would be folly. Civilized races were not the only ones addicted. When the Visigoths besieged Rome, they extracted among other ransom a substantial quantity of pepper. By the end of the Middle Ages, European demand, and consequently the price, became so great that pepper was sometimes called "black gold." Among the most venerable trade guilds was that of the Pepperers, sometimes also called *grossarii,* which has given us the word *grocery.*

Arab merchants controlled the supply of pepper and other spices until the sixteenth century. Not only did they monopolize trade routes, they were masters of propaganda. Even learned classical writers such as Herodotus were gullible enough to believe their fantastic tales about the sources of spices and the dangers involved in obtaining them. Cinnamon sticks, it was said, were used to build the nests of huge, menacing birds around the Red Sea who fortuitously dropped them onto the water to be collected by intrepid boatmen. Ginger was cultivated by troglodytes living in caves protected by vicious serpents. These myths may have justified exorbitant prices for a while, but slowly it occurred to the commodity traders of the late Middle Ages that it was imperative to get directly to the sources. When it came to spice, price truly was no object. Nothing encourages fashionable people to accept a new food quicker than rarity and costliness. And nothing is better for business than snobbery harnessed to novelty.

Unlike today, a healthy social emulation once worked soundly, and people strove to imitate their "betters." Spices represented all that was cultivated, elegant, and refined; that is, all that conjured the culturally advanced Arab-Islamic world. Spices also tasted good, and

Shakers, or casters, were an early form of spice dispensers. Spices also had religious significance; on the right is a besamim box, or spice tower, used in the Jewish Habdalah ceremony. In back is an eighteenth-century oyster-veneered walnut spice box.

More than four thousand years ago, people ground spices on rough stones. An English Edwardian ebony and silver pepper grinder was an elegant alternative.

It was the height of luxe to offer one's guests a variety of spices at the table. Cumin, pepper, and saffron were so desirable that they were treated like expensive jewels. The French turned-walnut box is from the late eighteenth century.

the medieval world hankered for strong flavors to cover up the signs of spoilage in their unrefrigerated foods.

Spices were also used as effective medicines and magical ingredients for alchemic experiments. It is not surprising, then, that elaborate vessels for the presentation of spices soon found a place in the worldly goods of grandees. At first they were improbable affairs, monumental towers that looked more like they belonged to the altar rather than the table, or tiny bejeweled boxes just large enough to hold a pinch of something.

As spices became part of the everyday culinary landscape, the objects designed for their domestic use reflected more modest practical concerns — special storage boxes of richly decorated tole or carved walnut usually fitted with locks. Handsome individual silver pepper pots survive from the seventeenth century. A variety of tools were used to grind spices, the mortar and pestle remaining the most common. Usually made of hard, nonporous materials like iron or marble, mortars were also fashioned in dense woods such as olive and box. Glass mortars were generally reserved for fine grinding of medicinal and aromatic spices. In the early nineteenth century, small pepper mills began to appear, and many were fancy enough to be used formally. They looked like miniature coffee grinders or chessmen with little gears, and were ornamented with polished woods and bound in silver or brass.

At table, spice was usually presented in a compartmentalized box with several sections, often with hinged lids. These chambered affairs accommodated several spices, usually pepper, salt, mustard, and cloves or cumin. Many examples of these survive in silver, porce-

Wet mustard has been popular in Dijon since the twelfth century. The silver French Empire-period moutardier *has its original blown glass liner. The spoon is Georgian.*

lain, faïence, ivory, and wood. A very early English silver spice box, possibly from the Tudor period, has six chambers, each with a hinged door.

Mustard, being the least expensive spice, became the most frequently served on everyday European tables. Originally offered in powder form, by the eighteenth century it was being made into a paste. The mustard pot by convention almost invariably took the form of a small barrel or tankard, and was usually accompanied by a condiment spoon that had an oval bowl. Lovely examples meticulously wrought in silver exist in large numbers. None, however, can compare to the one that once belonged to Madame de Pompadour and is now at the Museum of Lisbon. This mustard barrel created by Antoine-Sébastien Durand in the 1750s is cradled in a little silver wheelbarrow held by cupids, and could be pushed around the table.

Spices were imbibed as often as they were eaten. The punch-drinking eighteenth century saw a vogue for a variety of spice graters. Particularly graceful little silver cylinders for nutmeg, with a compartment for the nut and a rough steel grate, found their way into the copious pockets of gentlemen's waistcoats or beside convivial punch bowls.

When the imperial reach of the European states assured that spices would be perpetually plentiful, some of the allure disappeared. That which had obsessed princes and impelled ships to sail unknown seas became exiled to a kitchen shelf. Paradise must promise fulfillment of impossible longings, not attainment of commonplace flavors. Culinary fashion suddenly decreed that the less a spice was noticed, the better it was. And so by the early decades of the twentieth century, cellars for salt and pepper and an occasional mustard pot were all that survived of the palate's most exotic and passionate flirtation. Such was not the case with sugar, whose popularity has remained uncontested.

The Egyptians embalmed with it, and the Byzantines overindulged in it, but, oddly, nutmeg was the last great exotic spice to be adopted in Europe. The silver Georgian graters were made in Birmingham, England, during the Regency period (early 1800s). The ebony and ivory grater is from the French Charles X period, circa 1820.

The most popular of all seasonings were salt and pepper; the most plentiful was mustard. The twentieth-century Art Deco set made from animal horn demonstrates the trio's enduring place on European and American tables.

sugar

Where or when did humankind not crave something sweet? Nowhere and never, it seems. If there is any proof of the common origin of species it is the universality of the sweet tooth. Ancients kept bees and stole their honey, and native North Americans boiled maple sap for syrup. Sugarcane, or more precisely its refined juices, finally so enraptured European and American palates that tabletop decor was altered and the histories of several continents were turned upside down.

Sugar cutting boxes, such as this early-nineteenth-century American example, were ingenious solutions for the frugal cook not wishing to waste a grain of the expensive stuff. The brass tongs are late eighteenth century.

Send boys abroad to foreign wars and they're bound to pick up loathsome habits. Crusaders who trudged along those caramel-scented roads to Palestine proved that. The few not killed, converted, or seduced came home hankering after many a pleasure of the infidel, not the least of which was sugar. Originally a grass native to India, it came to Persia and eventually found its way into the busy trade routes of the Arab world. In Sanskrit, sugar was called *sarkara,* meaning "pebble." The word was lazily translated into Arabic as *sukkar* and has kept this basic sound no matter what language tried to reinvent it.

Supply was short, but by the tenth century, Venice, that clearing-house of everything deluxe, had depots of the stuff and resold it at great price. Cane later found its way to the Balearic Islands off the coast of Spain, but production was limited, and sugar remained one of the world's most expensive condiments. When Boccaccio sought to dramatize conspicuous consumption, he depicted privileged nobles existing mainly on a diet of sweets.

Meant for serious cracking, large sugar nippers were often mounted on boards to give greater leverage and stability. These are English, circa 1790.

Tongs and mallets were part of the torturous-looking arsenal used to prepare sugar for its more glamorous uses.

Sugar bowls came in every imaginable size and shape. These porcelain examples show the variety of decoration lavished on the form.

Before his famous transatlantic cruise, Christopher Columbus, who had been transporting sugar from his mother-in-law's Madeira estate to the busy markets of fifteenth-century Genoa, got interested in exploration. On his second New World venture, his crew planted some European cane in Hispaniola. It flourished, and within a generation, sugar was being exported to Europe, creating vast new fortunes. African slavery and the struggle of European powers for a foothold in the Caribbean became inexorably tied to sugar cultivation.

Meanwhile, housewives, taste setters, cooks, and craftsmen went on a three-hundred-year-long spree to indulge and display their sweet tooth. Sugar consumption grew apace with drinking tea, chocolate, and coffee and with an emerging complicated new cuisine that included dramatic developments in the pastry chef's art. It was no stunning news when at the beginning of the nineteenth century, Brillat-Savarin pronounced that sugar had become the "universal condiment" and claimed more money was spent on it than bread.

In its refined state, sugar came in several forms. There were crystals much favored by apothecaries; an expensive highly refined sugar that was powdered; and solid cones, or "loaves," the most fragile of which were called *cassonade* (from *casser*, "to break") or *crac* in French. Loaf sugar had to be broken up into lumps or pounded into granules to be used for teatime or dessert. These procedures required a range of torturous-looking equipment. Iron nippers resembling oversize pliers with flattened blades were used to crack up sugar cones. Larger models were mounted on wooden planks in order to stabilize the cutting action, or in open boxes to catch the sugar as it was broken up for domestic use. When powdered or granulated sugar was desired, various mallets pounded the nipped chunks into a fine dust.

The earliest sugar containers were small boxes that probably held crystallized forms meant for eating. There are French references to covered sugar bowls as early as the sixteenth century, but none survive. Very probably their shape was suggested by Chinese porcelain tea articles. A century later, fancy sugar equipment began to appear everywhere in Europe. Made in silver, glass, and porcelain, the form followed contemporary trends in design. Because sugar was

These Georgian antique sugar casters indicate how grand sprinkling sugar had become. The beautifully pierced French silver sifter spoons offer a more modest alternative.

Sugar tongs first followed the form of scissors or nips. Their practical purpose did not interfere with great whimsy of expression. The harlequin with hoops was made in London in 1905. The decorative acorn nips, London, 1854, are quite rare by today's standards.

a very expensive luxury, sugar dishes were small and usually had a top. The accompanying spoons were often distinguished by a slightly larger bowl which, like scoops for tea caddies, often employed a shell motif.

A fashion for sprinkling sugar through a sieve or strainer to create a powdered effect encouraged the development of two other types of sugar servers. Sugar casters, used to dispense a powdered sugar for fruits, pastries, and perhaps some beverages, made their appearance during the later part of the seventeenth century in

France, and were quickly adopted in England and on the Continent. This cylinder-shaped container had perforations in the lid and may have inspired the later salt shaker, which it resembled. Much creativity was brought to bear on their design, and lovely casters were made in porcelain as well as silver. A gigantic one belonging to a service made for Louis XIV around 1680 by Nicolas de Launay is in the Nationalmuseum in Stockholm. English silver examples, of which a great many survive, achieved their most graceful expression during the late Georgian period and are particularly attractive to collectors.

Sugar sifter spoons appeared almost simultaneously with the caster. They were rather like sauce ladles with bowls elaborately pierced to allow for scattering crushed sugar. Both the caster and spoon were popular for two centuries and were still part of table equipment in Europe in the early twentieth century.

By 1760 a particularly English fashion for sugar baskets became popular. Made in silver or Sheffield plate, they had glass liners and were used especially during the tea service. Although the idea was adopted in continental Europe, European baskets never reached the refinement of English work.

During the nineteenth-century, when Empire and neoclassical taste reigned, sugar receptacles tended toward the monumental and theatrical. Often resembling sauce tureens on elevated bases, they were sometimes outfitted with slots for spoons. Presenting so much expensive cracked sugar in such an extravagant manner was a statement of status.

By this time almost all table sugar was in lump form, requiring larger bowls. Where sugar was served in this way, pincers or tongs were more convenient than spoons. The ingenuity brought to bear in the design of sugar tongs, the grace and variety of their decoration, and especially the vast numbers of surviving eighteenth-century examples testify to how elegant and broadly observed the rituals of sugar were.

Freed from many strict functional requirements, sugar containers took every whimsical shape imaginable: melons, shells, flowers, fruits, tortoises, and griffins have all been pressed into service to hold and serve what few could or wished to resist.

Holiday cakes, such as the bûche de noël *(Yule log), were often presented with ceremony. The Georgian salver is eighteenth-century, and the English knife is nineteenth-century.*

cake

The story of sugar wouldn't be complete without noting its alliance with the dramatic developments in the pastry chef's art, which reached its apogee in the nineteenth century. Creams and soufflés played their part, but cake was the crowning glory.

By the end of the eighteenth century, the French were willingly submitting to the tyranny of chefs while busily overthrowing timid monarchs. The fickle relationship between crown and cake is

nowhere better expressed than in the ill-timed remark by that mis-understood queen, Marie-Antoinette. It seems most likely that she was quoting a passage from Jean-Jacques Rousseau's immensely popular book, *Confessions,* which had been published a few years earlier. And though what she said has been translated as "let them eat cake," she would have used the word *brioche,* a yeasty bread, not *gateau,* meaning cake. The guild system since the late Middle Ages had strictly limited the scope of the pastry maker to creations of

Wedding cakes have an ancient lineage. As cakes became more elaborate, so did the trays used to support them.

Edwardian silver-plated cake stands were common devices in England for passing dainties around. Silver baskets usually held petits fours or muffin-shaped cakes rather than cake slices.

baked goods containing butter, eggs, and sugar. But by the eighteenth century a "cake" could be almost anything that was round and baked.

The Israelites may have discovered how to make dough rise or may have learned it during a happy moment of their captivity. Inordinately fond of bready foods, Egyptians left hieroglyphic lists of more than forty cakes and breads they fancied. But it is to the Greeks we owe the development and refinement of baking. Their invention, the oven with movable front doors, has essentially remained unchanged since the seventh century. Greeks plied their trade in Italy and taught the Romans how to bake. Greek cakes were not the fluffy things we think of now, but more likely resembled the sweet-meats of North Africa, with layers of pastry crust soaked in honey, oil, and wine and stuffed with nuts and seeds.

Until the middle of the seventeenth century, the chief form of cake or pastry was the torte, a flaky pastry shell with removable top crust that could be filled with anything and usually was. For desserts it was filled with creams or candied fruits. During the next hundred years the scene changed rapidly. Abundant sugar was available from colonial enterprises, chocolate and coffee had become established facts of life, and an ever expanding privileged class could enjoy the pleasures of not only an ample table but a refined one. Chefs in private houses and in the new public restaurants were encouraged to vie with one another to produce wondrous confections. A few great chefs even created masterpieces that changed the very idea of dessert.

Without question, the nineteenth century was the era when people of all ranks ate cake. Except in the most abject huts, cakes large and small graced buffets and tea tables. For households too busy or too inept to create them, the village pastry shop provided a daily display of astounding variety. Even in eighteenth-century America, great confectioners were open for business in Boston, Philadelphia, and Charleston.

Holidays have always been marked by special foods and in most instances a cake defines the festivity. Christmas in the English world means fruitcake and gingerbread and on the Continent a *bûche de noël*. In Christian Europe and its colonies, Epiphany, or Twelfth

Night, was unthinkable without its King cake containing a bean. The wedding cake, which had been a tradition in the Renaissance, almost died out until it reappeared in the late eighteenth century. Cakes became so important to entertaining that wise housekeepers were drawn to recipes that promised cakes of enduring shelf life. Cake boxes and cake covers became essential equipment for protecting freshness.

The silver cake basket became an important element of the table's decoration as well as being used to pass queen's biscuit, seed-cakes, macaroons, and marchpane (marzipan). The earliest cake

The porcelain Derby and Spode plates are early nineteenth-century. The late-eighteenth-century square dish is from a Paris factory. The nineteenth-century tole cake box was a useful and attractive way to keep cake fresh.

Eighteenth-century dessert services were rarely designed to match dinnerware and were therefore much more decorative.

baskets appeared in the middle of the eighteenth century. Porcelain dessert services, usually lavishly decorated and rarely matching dinner services, incorporated a number of dishes and footed stands to present dainty cakes. Like the cakes themselves, these dishes were often heart, diamond, or club shapes, a style greatly favored for cake molds, along with "turk's caps" and squared cylinders.

A trowel-like implement appeared about the same time as cake baskets. It usually had a triangular-shaped blade that was often pierced and was used for cutting and serving "great" cakes. The early examples are almost indistinguishable from the very similar fish slice. Smaller versions of this implement which looked more like miniature shovels were used for petits fours and appeared only in the early nineteenth century. A fancier and more diminutive version of the carving knife meant for cake cutting also appeared around 1850. These are easily identified because their blades are serrated and often silver-plated.

As the nineteenth century progressed, cookbook writers in England, America, and France devoted increasing numbers of pages to the subject of cakes and extorted ever more complicated feats from the kitchen. Antonin Carême, author of the most influential cookbooks of that century, became the doyen of French *"grande cuisine."* He pronounced on all things gustatory, and in his *Patissier pittoresque* (The Artistic Pastry Chef, 1842) enumerated the true arts of man. This most literate of chefs praised music, poetry, literature, painting, and finally architecture, of which, he declared, pastry was perhaps its greatest expression. Making great cakes, like making beautiful buildings, requires that which we have little of today: faith in the future, a grasp of the past, and a sense of proportion. Like a taste remembered but lost, both seem to belong to the kitchens and drawing boards of yesterday.

Copper and tin cake molds were essential equipment in every well-stocked nineteenth-century European and American kitchen.

CHAPTER *6*

in their cups

Totally unknown to Europe before the sixteenth century, three exotic beverages came from the far corners of the earth not only to change what and how we ate, but to generate more glamorous equipment than any other food innovation ever had.

By the end of the seventeenth century, a number of crank-and-gear devices had been developed to grind the coffee bean. While some elegant Turkish and European models have survived, most were utilitarian, like this French walnut-and-iron example, circa 1700.

tea

Tea is so ancient we have no way of knowing the plant's certain origins. Because it grows wild on the slopes of Assam, it may have been brought to China by itinerant scholars like Gan Lu, who traveled to India in the second century, returning with tea and the tenets of Buddhism. Later it was carried in the begging bags of Chinese monks who went as missionaries to Japan. It has always had spiritual and decorative associations, but how men were inspired to brew it was the subject of argument. Confucian chronicles claim the notion was given to the Chinese at the time of creation by a descendant of one of the twelve Emperors of Heaven. However, the version involving Bodhidharma, a sixth-century Buddhist saint who once fell asleep during one of his epic prayer vigils, is more compelling. Having awakened, Bodhidharma was so disgusted with such backsliding he chopped his eyelids off and tossed them on the ground.

Originally, Europeans copied Chinese practice and drank tea out of bowls, but by the mid-eighteenth century, cups with handles were popular.

Miraculously, they took root and grew into a tea bush overnight. The astonished monk threw a few leaves into some boiling water, brewed the first tea, and saint and sinner alike have been kept awake by the stimulating power of this drink ever since.

The first reliable written references to tea occurred in a Chinese text dating from 50 B.C. Exact chronology is complicated by the variety of written characters used to represent tea. The *Cha Jing,* the oldest treatise on the subject, was composed by Lu Yu, an eighth-century circus performer turned scholar. He instructs not only on how to select, prepare, and serve tea, but describes the utensils as well. Even by this time tea was more than a beverage that healed or soothed but a social art as well. The tea ceremony largely formed by the Zen aesthetic emerged as an integral part of the culture of Japan in the tenth century. Among other things, it put great emphasis on the implements used for taking tea. They were chosen for their rustic simplicity and spontaneity of form. Kettle, caddy, bowl, and brazier all assumed supreme importance, an influence that would be later felt in drawing rooms and cozy parlors from Dublin to Danzig.

Marco Polo, who commented on almost everything else, made no mention of tea in his travel accounts of the late thirteenth century. Yet less than two hundred years later, tea was known to Europeans, mainly sailors and intrepid travelers. In 1559 the Venetian geographer Giovanni Battista Ramusio was the first to report a tale told by Persian merchants about the Chinese habit of drinking tea and its benefits to health and long life. After that, the story began to unfold rapidly. Observant Jesuits, mainly Portuguese, took note of the habit and published several accounts. Overcoming any Reformation scruples about reading works by their archenemies, the Dutch turned the information to their own commercial advantage. A race was on for the exploitation of Eastern markets.

Fashionable Europeans of this period could be sold anything that promised to alleviate gout or serve as an aphrodisiac. Oddly, the French, who instinctively embraced nearly every culinary novelty, tended to intellectualize tea. First they tried it, then condemned it, relented, and debated it endlessly in the Faculty of Medicine of the Sorbonne. Finally so much dust had been raised over the matter that the king, Louis XIV, ordered his physician Nicolas de Blegny to investigate. By 1687 his resounding affirmation of all its properties in the definitive *Le Bon usage du café, du thé et du chocolat* insured its acceptance in society.

For the English it was simpler. Anything naughty or profitable promptly became fashionable, and at first tea was both. Of course, its early popularity might be explained in part by the English habit of adding a dash of spirits to the brew. Tea eventually became one of England's main economic fuels and a virtual symbol of Empire. By 1657, tea was being advertised in Garway's London coffeehouse. Three years later, Samuel Pepys was confiding to his diary that he had tasted his first cup of "tee." With this, the English commenced a

The English probably made the first silver pot specifically for tea in the late seventeenth century. This heavily worked example is from the William IV period (1830–37), and the tea strainer is late-nineteenth-century French.

romance that would last seemingly forever. A century later, Samuel Johnson admitted to drinking up to twelve cups at a sitting and to being "a hardened and shameless tea drinker." Moral reformers espoused tea for the "lower orders" as a substitute for their pints, and socialites like Anna, Duchess of Bedford, enshrined it as a late-afternoon ritual. Even America's national identity became inexorably bound up in the substance, as our revolution was forged at a "tea party."

At first much of the publicly served tea in Europe was stored like ale in barrels and gulped out of tankards and posset cups by the rougher clientele of coffeehouses. The more genteel drinker followed the Chinese custom of brewing small quantities of fresh tea by pour-

Teatime required elaborate equipment, such as this early-nineteenth-century French rolled-plate silver urn.

Tea tables, such as this mahogany example, were initially inspired by old Chinese tea trays and were often designed with a tray top or a gallery.

ing boiling water directly over leaves in tiny porcelain bowls. The bowls were often exported along with the tea, packed tightly among the leaves in the tea chests.

Despite an insatiable lust for porcelain among European collectors, for a long time the secrets of its manufacture eluded them. The first European pots made specifically for brewing tea were metal and probably English. Their shapes were modeled on Chinese examples, either spherical or pear-shaped, and soon were fitted with a strainer in the spout. The earliest known silver teapot of this type is engraved with a date of 1670. Within a few decades, similar vessels were being made in Holland and France. It seems curious that the French did not begin to strain the spout until much later. There is a very early American-made silver teapot surviving from 1701. The first complete silver tea service of numerous matching pieces was made in Augsburg, Germany, around 1720. Later, as taking tea became more ritualized, the Russian samovar was adapted by Europeans. By the end of the eighteenth century, the hot-water urn in silver, pewter, or decorated tole became the most monumental piece to be included in the tea service.

With the development of porcelain factories in France and Germany at the beginning of the eighteenth century, lavish tablewares were produced. Because holding a bowl full of a hot liquid required too much dexterity and patience, the idea of a cup with a loop handle was quickly adopted, and by 1760 the teacup with handle had come to dominate the fashion in Western tea wares.

The first ceramic teapots from the factories of Saint-Cloud and Dresden were completely of Chinese inspiration and decoration. While French and German artisans produced beautiful examples of silver pots, many of these were for export because their countrymen continued to prefer tea brewed in porcelain pots. Of all the new foods and culinary fashions introduced to Europe from the seventeenth century onward, none challenged craftsmen and inspired more paraphernalia than tea. Purveyors of luxury wares immediately perceived the potential in this new beverage. The number of grandees portrayed at the tea table in eighteenth- and nineteenth-century paintings demonstrates how quickly tea became one of the chief emblems

The French and Germans were the first Europeans to master the Chinese techniques of hard-paste porcelain. This Vieux Paris, or Old Paris, tea set is circa 1840.

of wealth, status, and refinement. Very quickly the tea table, either round or square, carved with a small gallery or "tray," became indispensable to a well-furnished room.

The freshness of these expensive leaves mattered greatly, and a connoisseurship of varieties and blends soon developed. Tightly lidded boxes for storing tea were created in silver and precious woods. These tea caddies often contained a small bowl for blending. A splayed-bowl caddy spoon also evolved, crafted in shovel or shell shapes. The latter mimicked the shells packed in with the leaves in the early crates of tea exported to Europe. The shells were used by the merchants in grading and sampling.

The variety of designs for teaspoons is astounding and forms its own category of collecting. For a time, the "mote" spoon was popular. This oddity had a long tapered handle with pierced bowl and pointed end, which was used to extract debris from a teacup and to free a clogged teapot spout. These implements became less popular with the introduction of small strainers and tea balls or infusers, which appeared in the first half of the nineteenth century.

Europeans added milk and sugar to their adopted beverage. Three hundred years later, in the early twentieth century, America made its own original contributions to tea culture. One was the addition of ice, which was introduced amid a heat wave during the St. Louis World's Fair in 1904; the other was the 1908 invention of the tea bag by New York tea importer Thomas Sullivan, which simplified and hurried the process. While the former invoked a new form of long-handled spoon, the latter contradicted the tempo and grace of a time-honored ceremony. A cup of tea, like love or a good cigar, takes time, and time is what we have left behind.

These nineteenth- and early-twentieth-century strainers were one way Europeans kept tea debris minimal.

Tea caddies became fancy affairs: an eighteenth-century English sterling silver caddy (left); a late-eighteenth-century English inlaid wood caddy; and an American sterling silver caddy, circa 1895.

chocolate

Despite the rumors, Montezuma was not a vengeful man. It seems he was a charming prince, a bit bewildered by ritual and prophecy, caught in one of those cyclonic moments only history can stir up. Much of the bad press came from guilty Spanish guests who abused the fifteenth-century Aztec ruler's lavish hospitality. Human sacrifice was just the drab part of his job. He much preferred an afternoon spent sipping bitter chocolate flavored with vanilla, cloves, and pepper. It was reported that Montezuma swilled upwards of fifty pitchers daily from a golden cup.

The conquistadors were single-minded — treasure and theology were one; so Aztec chocolate as well as gold and pagan souls came back as booty in the holds of galleons homeward bound. The gold was flaunted, misspent, and lost; the souls — who knows? The chocolate, however, they hoarded, for it bewitched all who drank it. The Spanish adopted native implements and techniques for preparation, but had the brilliant idea of adding sweetening.

Within a century, Spanish ladies were so addicted to their cocoa that they carried cups and pots and *molinetes*, wooden whisks, right into church. Soon the sipping and frothing taxed the patience of the unusually tolerant dear old Archbishop of Mexico. Finally he prohibited colonial ladies and their maids from drinking during worship. Underestimating the furies, he was soon sent to an untimely reward — poisoned by his own morning cup of chocolate. The lesson was not lost on higher prelates. Perhaps fearing further retribution from the devoted, Rome proclaimed that chocolate did not break the fast.

Despite Spanish efforts to keep secret bean and recipe, both soon were known from Antwerp to Vienna. Luxury-loving monks fed in Spanish convents tucked little sticks of chocolate into ample sleeves and carried them to confreres across Europe. It was not long before the Continent, cloistered and uncloistered, thought of little else.

Louis XIV's young wife Marie-Thérèse added to her retinue a servant whose only task was making daily cups of chocolate. A taste for the expensive elixir swept through the most fashionable circles in France and became a mania. Perhaps the only pause in this exhilaration occurred after an unsettling incident rather breathlessly reported by Madame de Sévigné in a letter to her daughter. The pretty

Two-handled cups, complete with lids, were especially useful for keeping the cocoa hot. These early-eighteenth-century Chinese chocolate cups are Kangxi and date to about 1700. Sèvres and Meissen made similar cups.

Marquise de Coetlogon, Sévigné wrote, had always partaken heavily of the drink and even more so during the boring days of her confinement. So when she birthed a cocoa-colored son, there was some mild alarm at court, and for a time chocolate was taken a tad more moderately.

It became clear that the three great beverages that hit Europe at the same time — coffee, tea, and chocolate — created a little revolution in style as well as refined habits. But there was definitely a ribald side to chocolate. Samuel Pepys, always abreast of the latest fad, had his first cup on a fine morning in 1662 in an infamous London "chocolate house" such as White's or the Cocoa Tree. There one could argue politics, flirt, play cards, and sip chocolate, all for a penny. William Hogarth, the eighteenth-century illustrator, left us a record of these places, and one suspects, quite rightly, that something more than ground beans went into those cups. Indeed wine, even rum, was used as often as water, making cocoa a somewhat more festive drink than we think of today. The beverage grew more genteel

Chocolate cups, such as this nineteenth-century Vieux Paris porcelain one, are taller and sit deeper in the saucer than coffee cups. Beneath the cup is a 1745 engraving of the cocoa bean by Johann Weinmann.

when a sober Spaniard or Englishman, we're not sure which, came up with the idea of using milk to mix it.

Early "medical" proponents of chocolate often claimed it was particularly helpful both in promoting amorous instincts and curing one of their consequent contagions. Madame de Pompadour relied heavily on it to warm her frigid blood before conjugal royal visits. Even Casanova found it a useful stimulant in pursuing his hobby across Europe.

In an age when people were still sensible, chocolate was thought to be a health food. Learned men proclaimed it an aid to digestion, weight control, and long life. At first it was dispensed from apothecaries, in little flat cakes or thin rolled sticks that would then be shaved or chopped for mixing. The first record of chocolate being sold in colonial America was in 1712 in Boston, by a pharmacist. And it was a doctor, James Baker of Dorchester, Massachusetts, who had the idea to "modernize" the arduous process of grinding cocoa beans with a mortar and pestle. Baker and his partner, John Hannon, began mechanically producing cakes of chocolate in 1765, starting a business still in operation today. Thomas Jefferson urged his countrymen to choose chocolate over tea. If they had listened, chocolate might have become the national drink.

Just observing how many portrait painters of the eighteenth century posed subjects with some kind of cup in their hands tells us how elegant and refined the habit seemed. But a certain provocative association lingered in the atmosphere around chocolate. The chocolate servers in the paintings of the eighteenth-century Swiss artist

A silver pot made in England about 1711 is one of the earliest examples from that country, where the sipping of chocolate was probably introduced by transplanted Dutch royals William and Mary.

Liotard are undeniably sensual. Nor could the portrait by Gautier-Dagoty of Madame du Barry saucily sipping cocoa be described as demure.

Because early chocolate was very dense, it required considerable whisking to create a liaison with the liquid it was mixed with. The Aztecs had prepared the concoction in clay pots, and early Spanish paintings show the Europeans did as well. Soon copper pots were used because they kept the heat and did not create an unfavorable reaction to the chocolate. They were sometimes crafted narrower

With the advent of less expensive powdered cocoa at the end of the nineteenth century, German as well as French factories began producing many fancy chocolate sets. This Continental porcelain set is probably from Bavaria, circa 1890.

6

7

1. A young Shoot.
2. Flower.
3. Ripe Fruit.
4. Ripe Fruit open.

5. Kernel
6. Kernel
7. Kernel

at the top to prevent splashing and were fitted with lids having a small aperture that would just accommodate the stem of the whisk and allow for its smooth rotation.

Among imaginative people, opulence, not form, follows function. Porcelain and silver makers of every country were quick to adapt to the fashion and produce chocolate sets of exceptional quality. Chocolate pots were usually identified by side handles and low spouts. Early chocolate cups adopted the form of a teacup but were somewhat taller and more conical. But given the popularity of the three beverages, there can be little doubt that pots and cups were interchangeable in all but the most fastidious or ostentatious households. By the 1750s, porcelain factories such as Meissen, Sèvres, and Bow were producing chocolate sets. The earliest chocolate pots in silver date from the late seventeenth century. At first, milk jugs often accompanied a chocolate pot. The type of cup most associated with chocolate is a two-handled affair with a deep saucer and often a cover, occasionally called a *trembleuse*. Early-nineteenth-century workbooks from Spode illustrate chocolate pots and cups that are remarkable for the richness of their decoration and their expense.

Common usage in culinary writing well into the nineteenth century interpreted chocolate to be only a beverage. The "chocolate cake" cited in Mary Randolph's classic nineteenth-century American cookbook refers to a cake to accompany the drink, not one flavored by it. "Eating chocolate," candy flavored by chocolate, was first widely marketed by an English company, Fry and Sons, in 1847.

By the end of the nineteenth century, a good-quality cocoa was being produced, and chocolate was being drunk at all times of the day. Social arbiters considered it the only proper alternative drink to serve at tea. Many of the handsomely decorated services from this period recall the distinctive early forms, with tall pots and high cups, and are exuberantly painted. These are usually Continental in origin.

Carolus Linnaeus, the Swedish naturalist, gave the cacao plant the botanical name *Theobroma* — Greek for "food of the gods." He could not anticipate that mortals, with their caprice and willfulness, would at last turn it into a food meant only to be resisted.

This rare miniature pot, like its full-scale prototype, has a small opening for the stem of a whisk.

coffee

Listening to Bach's lovely Coffee Cantata (1732), we sense something is not quite right. The young Liesgen suddenly protests that her morning brew is better than a thousand kisses. This eligible fraulein defies her father and risks disgrace and spinsterhood rather than kick her coffee habit. Well, honestly, who has not felt that way from time to time? But the sentiment is a bit unsettling coming at the threshold of the Romantic Age. It hints at how far Europe had come to regard this new beverage.

Coffee, sometimes called the wine of Islam, was apparently native to Abyssinia (now Ethiopia), where it grew wild. First used as a foodstuff, the beans were crushed and rolled with fat into what must have been a rather revolting little bonbon. Traders from Yemen introduced the bean to the vibrant world of the Middle East, and by the eighth century there are references to the medicinal uses of coffee in Arabic texts. It was said to have cured the Prophet of narcolepsy. As we have seen, he was not the only holy man to have a problem with dozing off during prayers. Because of its stimulating properties, coffee offered teetotaling societies an ideal substitute for alcohol and wine. Muslim bons vivants, looking for some convivial drink to while away hot afternoons, experimented with various methods of roasting and grinding coffee beans. Nevertheless, it does not seem to have been brewed seriously until the fifteenth century. Around 1620 it was imported to Europe through Venice. When Europeans were taking their first sips of the stuff, both Cairo and Istanbul had more than a thousand coffeehouses.

It didn't take long for coffee to become far and away the favorite and most controversial of the three beverages that spilled into Europe around the same time in the seventeenth century. Chocolate was too heavy and rich to be drunk all day, and tea became just a mite too polite. Coffee, on the other hand, had a vaguely exciting and disreputable air. That charming French treatise of 1687, *Le bon usage du café, du thé et du chocolat,* insisted that, among other benefits, coffee was a cure for some of the more pestiferous *maladies d'amour.* Despite the failure of these early promises, by 1700 there were several thousand coffeehouses in London, and as many in Paris. The fashion was taken up with a vengeance in Vienna, where the Turks had been defeated, their

The enamel drip coffeepot was standard kitchen equipment by the 1870s, as shown by the tall 1910 American version by Bigelow, Kennard and Co., Boston.

bags of coffee confiscated, and coffee drinking became the national sport of both sexes. Even in America, usually unfashionably late with every new culinary trend, coffeehouses prospered.

Initially coffeehouses were bawdy male clubs where ladies, if not women, were excluded. They functioned as centers of gossip, political discussion, sedition, business negotiation, and literary inspiration. It was no coincidence that one of the first coffeehouses in London was established by Edward Lloyd, who, after eavesdropping on a merchant's talk of shipping news, also established an insurance company that became renowned. Benjamin Franklin ran a coffeehouse in connection with his Philadelphia printing shop, and the Boston Tea Party was hatched at the Green Dragon, which was a local coffee — not tea — house. It didn't take long for coffee to

Large commercial grinders, like the 1885 example from the Enterprise Manufacturing Company of Philadelphia, were used in general stores and cafés.

When the first cylinder roaster was invented in 1650, variations quickly followed. An early-nineteenth-century pan-and-paddle model was convenient for stovetop use.

Turkey's attachment to coffee shows up in its ornate antique brass pots and grinders. The nineteenth-century French cups are a form that originated in North Africa for serving the sweetened coffee called mazagran.

Like tea, coffee was originally drunk from ceramic bowls without handles, and the fashion for drinking morning café au lait in bowls still endures in the French countryside. These ceramic bowls are early twentieth century, as is the French enamel pot.

invade the privileged drawing room as well, and the great number of paintings depicting the smart set drinking coffee confirms its rapid domestication.

The challenges involved in coffee preparation remained basically the same for a thousand years: how to roast the beans without burning them, how to grind them without damaging them, and how to serve the drink efficiently and elegantly. Beautifully executed braziers, small brass mills for grinding, and high-spouted pots for brewing were being made from the Nile to the Bosporus by 1500. Many Turkish gentlemen carried their own grinders as part of their everyday gear. Two centuries later some of this equipment was making its way to France via Marseilles, and Amsterdam. At first Europeans used mortars and pestles to pulverize the beans. One such mortar survives from the *Mayflower*. It belonged to the parents of the first colonial child born in New England, Peregrine White.

In the earliest times, roasting was done over the open hearth in flat iron or pottery pans. By the end of the seventeenth century the technology had begun to improve. A cylinder roaster made of tin was invented in England in 1650, and refinements quickly followed. This method allowed the beans to be tossed during roasting, thus pre-

venting scorching and its unpleasant aftertaste. Small roasters became standard kitchen equipment and remained so for more than two hundred years, being used well into the early twentieth century. The skills of the tinsmith were applied to a variety of forms, ranging from large commercial roasters to small ones that would fit on the open eye of a coal stove, producing just enough for a household.

Politics and cuisine are often dished out of the same pot. The visit of the Turkish ambassador Soliman Aga to the court of Louis XIV in 1669 created a craze among the fashionable classes for all things Turkish: cushions, turbans, and, of course, coffee. Not everyone was susceptible. The Duchesse d'Orleans writing from Marly in July 1704 confessed that she could drink neither tea nor chocolate nor coffee. "All this foreign stuff," she confessed, "is repugnant to me and . . . in this respect as in many others I can not be *à la mode*." When it comes to being chic, most French waste no time or energy. They borrowed a few ideas from the Italians, and soon were making fairly sophisticated crank-and-gear coffee grinders. These rarely reached the extravagant levels of Ottoman models, which sometimes employed precious materials and were sometimes jewel-encrusted; however, many French examples did have handsomely carved walnut

The European infatuation with coffee was linked to the high style of its service. This collection of eighteenth- and nineteenth-century pots reflects a range of styles and tastes. The taller silver vessel is an extremely rare American pot by Otto Paul de Parisien. The unusual English spoon warmer at left is one of a pair, circa 1870.

bodies with small drawers to capture the grounds. As France and Holland developed coffee-producing colonies, more and more related paraphernalia was manufactured. The early grinders are rare and highly prized, but even the later nineteenth-century ones from companies such as Peugeot, with their ingenious geared mechanisms, command large prices and are marvelous examples of engineering.

In Turkey the finely ground coffee bean was boiled in water and served from the same vessel, often of brass or steel. At first the same technique was adopted in Europe, and early coffeepots were on feet to allow a small spirit lamp to be placed under them. Unlike the teapot, which had a relatively low-slung spout, the coffeepot from the beginning had the spout placed as high as possible, sometimes being only a beak, to allow the grounds to settle. This high spout became the coffeepot's distinguishing characteristic.

At the end of the eighteenth century, the inspired Monseigneur Jean-Baptiste de Belloy took time off from his minor duties as Archbishop of Paris and invented the filtered system of making coffee. Inspired by the Venetians, he placed the ground coffee in a pierced tin cup on top of a pot and dripped hot water through the cup, producing a more delicate drink. This device was continually improved upon but never superceded. Most important, it allowed the preparation to be separated from the presentation.

The imperative of style is the most impatient of instincts, and one rarely constrained by practicality. Almost simultaneously the first silver coffeepots were introduced in Paris and in London around 1672. Soon accompanying spoons, milk jugs, and cups, which were usually smaller than teacups, appeared. The love of coffee unleashed several centuries of creativity, expressed in lavish designs of silver, porcelain, faience, enamelware, and painted tole. As coffee moved from the privileged classes to the mass market during the nineteenth and twentieth centuries, popular graphics and designs were ingeniously worked into packaging and advertising. Madame de Sévigné, that seventeenth-century writer and lady of fashion, once high-handedly dismissed coffee as a craze that would last but a generation.

The first standard silver set is from eastern France, circa 1860. The distinguishing characteristic of a coffeepot, as compared to a teapot, is a highly placed spout or beak.

At first, coffee was boiled and pots sat on feet so that spirit lamps could be placed under them. The idea of inserting a spigot in a coffee urn was probably first tried in Holland in the early eighteenth century. This Dutch painted-tole pot is circa 1800.

CHAPTER 7

the *enchantments*
of the *c*ommonplace

Little Mademoiselle Bertin, milliner to Marie Antoinette, once exclaimed to her demanding client that there was nothing new except what has been forgotten. Cuisine, like hats, bears witness to this bon mot. The egg, asparagus, and oyster are all as old as humankind itself, yet, rediscovered, have found privileged places in the new cuisine. Their timeless appeal was registered on the palate and the palette; for centuries still-life artists exalted these three foods. Presenting them has inspired beautiful, even fanciful tableware. It is not just their textures that have sparked the imagination but the memories they evoke as symbols of everyday abundance.

eggs

The ordinary life of princes is always a spectacle, occasionally scandalous, and in rare moments even stylish. So when that self-indulgent monarch Louis XV sat for his Sunday breakfast, he drew a crowd. They came to watch him take a boiled egg, slice off the end with one mighty whack of his knife, and dig in. We are not sure whether he invented the egg spoon or whether he merely grabbed a convenient mustard spoon whose shape seemed well suited to the task. It is likely that his own eggcups were no less grand than the ones executed by the great French silversmith François-Thomas Germain, now on exhibit in the National Museum of Ancient Art in Lisbon. By no means did Louis Quinze invent egg-eating, although it had been thought a trifle plebeian before he cast majestic glamour on the practice. He and his fashion-conscious mistress Madame de Pompadour kept prize laying hens in the attics of Versailles and made the consumption of this simple food quite chic. For the next 250 years, until the doomsday dietitians of our own times proclaimed against them, princelings and fastidious commoners alike sought to acquire all sorts of richly crafted accoutrements for the enjoyment of eggs.

The egg may have been known before the chicken, at least in Europe. In fact, chickens appeared rather late on the menu, not showing up in Greece until around the fifth century B.C., presumably having escaped their natural habitat in the Malaysian jungle and scratched their way across India and Persia, finally to be adopted in the ancient Mediterranean world. Ducks were the first domesticated fowl in China at least four thousand years ago. Their eggs were venerated. The Egyptians were not far behind. If the ciphers on the stela of Sehetep-Ab are correct, Pharaoh's men swept marshy reaches of the Nile to bag a type of migratory duck that had both gustatory and religious significance. For ancients, the egg became a symbol of fertility and of transformations. Because most birds cease laying eggs in winter, the resumption of this phenomenon was linked to early spring and the rebirth of nature. These notions eventually found their way into the profound Christian metaphors of resurrection and redemption represented by the Easter season.

The skillful Romans raised chickens and developed rather clever systems of incubation, but they preferred the critter primarily for sacrificial rather than culinary purposes. Apicius includes eggs in recipes without any particular emphasis on them. We know that in the fifth century, Clovis, king of the Franks, was so inordinately fond of hard-boiled eggs he lived in a perpetual state of indigestion which even his learned Byzantine doctor could not cure. The first large-scale commercial egg producer may have been Charlemagne, who in the eighth century raised chickens on his estates and sold the eggs profitably.

The presentation of grand and exotic egg dishes at medieval banquets tended to be ceremonial, but unfortunately we have no

Egg-eating has inspired almost as many inventions as wine-bottle opening. This late-nineteenth-century Russian steel double cup provided for convenient traveling with its built-in slicer.

record of any special serving pieces created for this purpose. Often the poor used eggs as a substitute for meat, but church worthies declared them unfit for consumption during Lent because they were essentially unrealized poultry.

This complicated canonical reasoning suggests the fascination eggs exerted over the mind of Christian Europe. Thirteenth-century accounts record the custom of English kings to have gold-leafed or colored eggs given as gifts during Easter. Apparently French rulers did the same. During the time of Louis XIV, pensioners of the Louvre were creating gorgeously decorated eggs that were presented to the king after Easter Mass. When the extravagant Russian goldsmith and jeweler Peter Carl Fabergé began creating his intricate and precious Easter eggs for Czar Alexander III in 1884, he was drawing on a venerable history.

Little evidence remains of how the simple egg was served at well-appointed tables before the eighteenth century, except for references to putting boiled eggs on folded napkins at each place. There are a few examples of curious silver German eggcups made in Augsburg around 1635, shaped like little boats or cradles that held an egg lengthwise instead of upright.

The earliest eggcup bearing the shape we recognize today is in the Metropolitan Museum; crafted by the French silversmith Pierre-Aymé Joubert around 1725, it looks like a miniature chalice. After this it seems that an hourglass form was generally adopted, although in Germany and some places in northern Europe, the taste for the sideways cup lingered. Sometimes individual porcelain cups were mounted on small trays that incorporated a saltcellar. Often these were produced in pairs, suggesting the boiled egg belonged to the intimate ritual of the breakfast meal. The English, especially, were partial to elaborate egg cruets, composed of a stand that would hold a number of removable eggcups, and sometimes small hooks for matching spoons.

By convention, egg spoons were either oblong or pear-shaped, making them convenient to run along the inside of the shell, and silver spoons often had gilded bowls. In nineteenth-century France, a spoon with an ivory or bone bowl and silver handle was used for eat-

The simplicity of the egg has fascinated human imagination and has had religious and metaphorical significance for thousands of years. Paradoxically, it has also inspired elaborate vessels for its presentation. This Old Sheffield egg cruet was passed around the breakfast table. The Irish Georgian spoons, circa 1780, are in the classic elongated oval shape.

ing eggs that had been coddled or shirred. There were porcelain and earthenware plates, designed much like oyster plates, for the presentation of hard-boiled eggs. Around 1850, boxed sets that contained an eggcup, spoon, and napkin ring became a favorite christening present among the affluent.

The fashion for egg-eating had grown so popular by the end of the eighteenth century that egg warmers or cookers in silver and tole became a rage that lasted well into the Edwardian period. These provided a fancy receptacle that would hold boiling water, fitted with a rack for submerging the eggs. Eventually some used alcohol burners

so the eggs could actually be cooked at the table. Around the 1780s, specialized scissors for cutting off the end of an egg began to appear. Like small guillotines on hinges, these objects were frequently created with fanciful decorations on the handle, sometimes suggesting the profile of a hen. It seems likely that this idea may have been modified for cutting the end off a cigar.

The great eighteenth-century philosopher Denis Diderot held up an egg, and suspecting it held the key to creation, predicted it would "overturn all the temples of the earth." Perhaps that was a little grandiose, but certainly it did have a powerful influence on what was in vogue for the well-appointed table.

In the early nineteenth century, boiling water was poured into the French painted-tole egg cooker before it was brought to the table.

An eggcup accompanied by a spoon was a favorite christening gift in the nineteenth century. This Napoleon III–period example is French first-standard silver. The exceptional egg cutter is English Georgian, circa 1790.

Elegant devices for the preparation of eggs at the table proliferated during the eighteenth century. This English silver-plate coddler stand, circa 1820, has a reservoir for boiling water to continue the cooking process in style.

Boiled eggs have been a culinary favorite in Europe since the Middle Ages. This late-nineteenth-century English majolica whimsy in the shape of a basket cradles a collection of hand-painted American milk-glass eggs decorated for Easter.

asparagus

Alas, we do not know what etiquette prevailed among the ancients for eating asparagus or whether any pretty table tools were developed for this purpose. The graceful Egyptians offered handsomely tied bundles to the gods, but did they eat them as well? When Pliny the Elder comments on an asparagus weighing more than a quarter of a pound, he seems neither surprised nor does he give particular instructions for cooking or eating it. How tantalizing to imagine that Romans used their fingers just as *à la mode elegantes* often do at the Ritz today. Apicius suggests that may be so. In a first-century recipe for cooking asparagus, he recommends two changes of water in order to keep the stalks firm. In other fragmentary recipes, however, we find him grinding them into a ghastly overspiced puree that one would need a spoon to eat.

To equate a love of asparagus with Civilization might be too much, but the barbarians seemed not at all fond of the vegetable — perhaps it was too effete for tribes busy pillaging. At any rate, it disappeared from mention for almost a thousand years. Certainly asparagus was eaten in the intervening centuries. Sensible people rarely forget a good dish, and asparagus continued to grow wild in warm hills from Provence to Tuscany. But it wasn't until the seventeenth century that it began to find its way back into recipe books.

Like all newly discovered foods in Europe, asparagus was believed to have aphrodisiac qualities, so naturally it was in great demand on princely tables. That royal glutton, Louis XIV, so craved it, his gardener devised a way to grow it in hothouses almost year round.

The king was less fond of the fork, which had been recently introduced to European courts from Venice, and preferred his fingers for asparagus. The satirist Thomas Artus, in *L'isle des Hermaprodites* (1605), thoroughly mocks fashionable people who pursued their peas and asparagus around their plates with silly forks. Hannah Glasse, who in 1747 wrote the most popular household book in English, *The Art of Cookery*, gives a recipe for asparagus that advises serving any sauce on the side to protect the hands from getting "greasy." This suggests that no good alternative had been found to the fingers or the useless fork.

Asparagus "eaters," such as these German silver ones, circa 1890, were preferred over forks. The sterling silver tongs are English Victorian.

The delicate colors of this French faience asparagus plate are typical of early-twentieth-century decorations from Sarreguemines.

In the second half of the nineteenth century, when industrialized silver production brought a host of little luxuries to a wider market, tables became littered with curious implements. The maddest and most challenging must have been the individual asparagus tongs, which were meant to grab an individual stalk and convey it to the mouth. One wonders how many diners, less than dexterous with dainty things, had shirt fronts or social careers ruined trying to use them. Sets in either silver or silver plate from the late nineteenth and early twentieth century are scarce but not rare. Their decoration suggests they were not made to match larger sets but were seen as optional service pieces. They are essentially miniaturizations of the larger serving pieces which have a much longer history.

Asparagus-serving tongs seem to be variations of the meat and sugar tongs made in England, France, and America since the second half of the eighteenth century. The larger versions of sugar tongs were made of one piece of silver bent into a tight U-shape that produced tension. There were also tongs with a spring action in the handles, resembling scissors. These are possibly the oldest versions, the narrower ones being used for steaks and the broader for asparagus.

The trompe l'oeil French "barbotine" plate circa 1870 shows how painterly and playful much of the late-nineteenth-century majolica wares could be. These compartmentalized majolica plates allowed for the variety of sauces popular with nineteenth-century bourgeois cuisine.

Later examples, which are quite short with very wide, flat lips, are now sometimes called sandwich tongs, but most nineteenth-century catalogs of manufactured silver pieces refer only to asparagus tongs. In the Victoria and Albert Museum, a manuscript from Garrard & Co., "goldsmiths and jewellers to the king," describes a pair of asparagus tongs made in 1776 by the well-known silversmith Thomas Chawner. The same source refers to the brothers Chawner supplying a five-pronged asparagus fork in the 1770s.

Asparagus has always been popular in prosperous households in America, and in the late eighteenth century everyone from Thomas Jefferson to the renowned hostess Mrs. Samuel Powel of Philadelphia grew it in their kitchen gardens, so these implements found their way onto elegant tables here as well.

A French barbotine cradle illustrates how playful decoration had become by the second half of the nineteenth century. It was a challenge for the cook to make the real thing just as pretty as the trompe l'oeil. Asparagus cradles often sat on platters with drainers, which allowed the dish to stay crisp and natural.

The history of the serving dishes is more difficult. The great era for ceramic and silver asparagus cradles and platters is indisputably the late nineteenth century. This is connected to the expanded demand by the respectable classes for elaborate refinements of the table. It is strange that no superb examples seem to exist from before this period. Among the amazing boiseries painted at the Château de Cormatin around 1620 there is a panel depicting a bunch of rather long, delicately colored white asparagus presented on a footed tazza. Was this an artist's conceit or a domestic hint? Unfortunately we may never know. Another panel in the same room shows fruit arranged on a similar stand, making any speculation inconclusive. The earliest reference to a platter explicitly for asparagus appears in the *Dictionnaire de l'Académie* of 1694. And the Musée des Beaux-Arts in Troyes has a slightly cratered pewter platter with holes for draining off excess water from cooked asparagus.

Factories such as Wedgwood in England and Creil and Gien in France produced a soft-paste creamware that was ideal for inexpensive but decorative table goods. Silver companies copied the notion in precious as well as inexpensive metal versions. Later the more whimsical and boldly colored majolica or, as the French called it, barbotine provided a vivid palette for the trompe-l'oeil depictions of asparagus and artichokes. Often these appeared as cradles with perforations set on platters sometimes including yet another draining plate that fit inside the platter. For collectors it is these charming pieces that are particularly interesting because beyond utility, they express the enthusiasm for this vegetable that has endured almost two millennia.

salad

It is during the fifteenth century that French treatises on cookery began including descriptions of raw vegetables and herbs sprinkled with oil and vinegar. By then the word *salad* had passed into the vocabulary of most modern languages from the Thames to the Danube. But the great era of salad making and salad serving began with the culinary transformations that took place in the second half of the seventeenth century. A well-known proverb of the period

quipped that a good salad required a miser for the vinegar, a spend-thrift for the oil, and a wise man for the salt. That useful gossip, the Duc de Saint-Simon, tells us that Louis XIV, with his Bourbon penchant for gluttony, consumed gigantic quantities of salad. Indeed so much, his dithering doctor, M. Fagon, and unrelenting wife, Madame de Maintenon, banished it from the table, causing the fashion to wane but not disappear.

Strainers and sifters were some of the earliest kitchen equipment. Glazed pottery forms with many perforations, such as the nineteenth-century French égouttoir, were essential in the cleaning and preparation of fresh vegetables and fruits.

The French salad grater was a convenient device that was indispensable in the preparation of shredded vegetables.

One of the oldest ways for formally presenting oil and vinegar is the handblown glass *guedoufle* from the early eighteenth century. By cleverly counterposing the spouts, each liquid could be poured separately from a single vessel. The late-nineteenth-century American silver-plated cruet stand includes receptacles for spices. The early-nineteenth-century French faience cruet set in a reticulated basket has holders for the stoppers, as does the silver and crystal set.

While handles might be made of silver, the bowls or tines of salad servers were usually produced in a material less sensitive to the corrosive effects of vinegar and salt, such as horn, ivory, or hardwoods.

After being washed, salad leaves were vigorously swung in wire-work baskets, which were the practical salad spinners of the nineteenth century.

About this time the first decorative objects associated with salad begin to appear. There are references to *saladiers*, bowls used for the preparation of salads, being part of kitchen equipment at the end of the seventeenth century. And oil-and-vinegar cruets make their debut. The earliest French examples are simple handblown glass affairs on a stand. By the eighteenth century, elaborate cruet stands were being produced in silver and crystal as well as porcelain and faience. Some of the most exuberant designs were lavished on these articles, and cruet sets remained popular everywhere for nearly three hundred years. Around 1750, ceramic table services began to regularly include a bowl for serving salads as well as smaller elongated serving dishes for relishes. Individual salad plates, however, appeared quite late in the process, as did specific serving implements. An enlarged fork and slotted spoon for the purpose were probably mid-nineteenth-century inventions associated with the proliferation of silver articles for the table. Like other specialty servers, they frequently were richly decorated and often had bowls and tines of ivory or horn to avoid damage by salty and acidic dressings.

half shells

Felix die! O happy day, when oysters piled so plentifully in the shallows of the seas that brimming baskets brought no amazement. For many coastal peoples they were a staple, not a luxury. Mountain-high middens confirm to archaeologists that for millennia, tribes with unwritten histories consumed tons of the briny bivalves. Furthermore, they seemed to have had the good sense to eat them only in cool seasons.

Page 97: A seaside fantasy under a gauze pavilion creates a sumptuous setting for an oyster supper. The French barbotine plates are circa 1890.

The painting "The Luncheon of Oysters" by Jean-François de Troy (1735) was destined for the private dining room of a young Louis XV. It captures perfectly the new mood of intimate dining in the period: camaraderie, minimal servants, equality at table, and the good cheer of a relatively new drink—champagne.

The very name we use today comes from the Greek word for the flat oyster shell, *ostrakon,* on which those early democrats scratched their votes or wrote names of politicians deemed undesirable enough to warrant exile. Thus giving the origin of our word *ostracism.* The fourth-century-B.C. poet Philoxenus of Cythera may have been the first to rhapsodize about fried oysters, which he enjoyed at a supper given by the Tyrant of Syracuse. Later, in almost every artistic allegory from the Renaissance to the twentieth century where Europeans sought to depict worldly abundance, oysters found a place on the canvas.

The busy Amerindians made little pomp of dining on the half shell, nor did the Romans who imported vast quantities of the shellfish from all over the empire, preferring those from Britannia. Their appetites produced astounding records of individual consumption and some revolting little tricks for relieving overindulgence, but no new gustatory equipment. Nor did any emerge over the ensuing centuries. If the delightful French aristocrat the Seigneur de Saint-Evremond was correct in claiming that there were more than four thousand oyster sellers in Paris at the end of the seventeenth century, why were no special implements or dishes created for the enjoyment of their wares? A marvelous painting by Jean-François de Troy from 1735 depicts a riotous luncheon of oysters in the private dining room of the young Louis XV. The jovial swains seated around the table appear much more concerned with sartorial refinements than culinary ones. The oysters had been carried into the sumptuous room in wicker baskets lined with straw. The plates and forks were the same as those used for eating anything. The only accompaniments were salt and bread and, of course, with great Gallic good sense, quantities of champagne.

A distinct oyster fork had to await the end of the century for its first timid general use. It may have been adapted by some enterprising host or hostess from the sharp, two-pronged sweetmeat fork long in use. There is a tantalizing picture in the Munich museum painted by Hendrick van Balen in 1610 that is part of a series on the four seasons. *L'hiver* (Winter) is an ermine-collared lady of ample bosom, *trés*

The jewel hones of these oyster plates is typical of the vibrant palette of English majolica manufactured in the second half of the nineteenth century.

décolleté. Before her are both candied fruit and oysters. Which, one wonders, is she preparing to eat with that small fork in her hand?

The earliest oyster forks, which are almost always French, have very slender handles of ivory or precious woods. The tines are often flanged on the outer edge to facilitate cutting the oyster's "eye" away from its shell. An exceptional set, circa 1820, in the collection of the Musée du Vieux Nîmes has a flat knife at one end and a small fork at

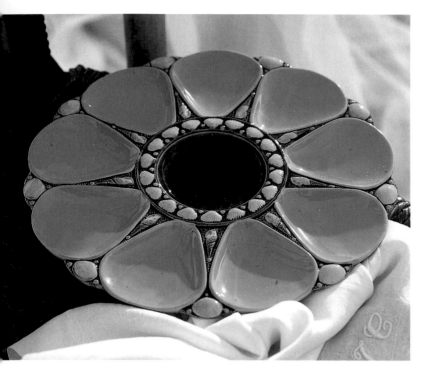

The jewel-like impression created by the smooth turquoise and pearled surfaces was typical of Minton ceramics in the 1870s and 1880s, a style copied by other English and American factories.

The nineteenth-century oysterman's basket holds early-nineteenth-century French ebony-and-silver oyster forks and imitation Minton plates from the 1880s.

George Jones, a nineteenth-century English potter, was known for plates with rich marine colors and sinuous encrustations of shells and seaweed.

the other, with a broad shaft of ivory for the handle. By the 1820s, hollow-handled silver forks appear as well.

Late-eighteenth-century English shellfish forks exist but are rarer. There is a surviving example by Hester Bateman from 1790 that has a flat solid silver handle and tines that are somewhat longer and larger than those of the French counterpart. Perhaps one reason English examples are scarce is that oysters were so common until the mid-nineteenth century that even Dickens's Mr. Pickwick remarked on the connection between poverty and eating oysters.

By the end of the nineteenth century, oyster forks were being incorporated into larger flatware sets, part of the trend toward mass-produced silverware and the vogue for expanding the battery of implements used to serve ever more complex cuisine and social table etiquette.

Perhaps the earliest example we have of a platter specifically designed for serving oysters is one made by the Sèvres factory

Early-nineteenth-century French ivory-and-silver oyster forks nestle in a turn-of-the-century Sarreguemines oyster plate. The color palette is softer than that of English products.

Spectacular oyster platters were among the earliest decorative oyster wares. The English ceramic stand in the foreground was made by Minton. The Napoleon III–period silver forks are examples of flatware that was considered necessary for a well-dressed table.

The painterly effects of these late-nineteenth-century porcelain oyster plates were a product of the Haviland company in Limoges, France. They suggest the trompe l'oeil taste of an earlier time.

around 1765. It is now in Florence in the Pitti Palace. A delicate tiered affair made of soft-paste porcelain, the naturalistic central column shaped like coral holds eighteenth small painted shells to present oysters. It is interesting that in the eighteenth century these objects are referred to in the Sèvres factory records as *étagère à coquilles,* or shelves of shells, and not until around 1840 are they referred to specifically as oyster plates. Such *présentoirs,* or servers, became popular items and were made in faience as well as porcelain. In England, Wedgwood was especially renowned for marine forms.

By 1860, innovative industrial processes and firing techniques provided a means for supplying the vast new markets with the ceramic tablewares demanded by the ever expanding prosperous middle classes in Europe and America. Elegant sets of individual oyster plates and serving platters were produced by the great porcelain houses. But it was especially the manufacturers of the tin-glazed pottery called majolica in England and barbotine in France who produced the most fantastical and amusing examples of this genre. The vivid colors of Minton and Wedgwood and the dashing designs of George Jones & Sons applied to oyster plates created a whimsy that practically submerged function. While a few American factories like Morley and Sons of East Liverpool, Ohio, produced majolica-type oyster plates, most were imported from England. In France, similar wares were made by Sarreguemines, Longchamps, and some of the older faience factories at Lunéville and Saint-Clement. In general, the French factories adopted a somewhat softer palette. Except for efforts to re-create the strong colors and dimensional forms of Palissy ware, French designs favored soft blues and pinks, melting yellows and seashore grays. The Continental plates leave the impression of being made primarily for culinary rather than decorative use.

The popularity of these wares lasted from 1860 through 1940, and then they passed out of vogue. These gorgeous accoutrements to a food that has been a favorite almost forever are a reminder of the fickleness of fashion and the fragility of nature. For the fresh oyster, like so many other simple things, has not fared well in the ecology of the modern world.

Opposite: The fascination with marine life inspired some of the earliest and most detailed zoological studies, such as these late-eighteenth-century English hand-colored engravings.

fish

Nutritious and plentiful, primal and mystifying, fish have been prized as foodstuffs and universally venerated as profoundly symbolic. Ancient civilizations used them as metaphors for fecundity, good fortune, longevity, eternal life, and the Divine itself. For this reason they are found as decorative motifs on almost everything humans have touched, from cave walls to mosaic floors.

The oval fish poacher called a poissonnière *(rear) and the* lozenge-shaped turbotière *have been standard kitchen equip-ment since the seventeenth century.*

In the late nineteenth century, porcelain sets for fish service adorned the fashionable table from Bavaria to Boston. The vivid coloring and 24-karat rims of this set are characteristic of Limoges china from the 1880s.

We know that fishing occurred all over prehistoric Europe and that the fish trade reached as far as Babylon. Alas, while much lore survives on the catching and cooking of fish, little is known about the evolution of stylish ways to present and eat it. Some clues can be found in artistic depictions and archaeological discoveries, however.

Quite early examples exist of special cooking equipment for fish preparation. A fish-shaped grill from the late Middle Ages is in

English majolica and French barbotine tin-glazed wares from the second half of the nineteenth century were often decorated with marine forms. This sardine dish and servers are English, circa 1885.

Huge numbers of exuberantly creative boxed fish services were produced by American silver manufacturers in the nineteenth century.

the collection of the Musée de Cluny. There are French citations for early fish-cooking pans called *poissonnières,* and the existence of a lozenge-shaped pan for the cooking of turbot is confirmed by a seventeenth-century inventory of the Archbishop of Bordeaux.

Special fish platters began to appear among eighteenth-century wares. These were often elongated ovals, made not only by the Meissen and Sèvres porcelain factories but also the more humble faience artisans. By the end of the nineteenth century, complete fish services adorned with elaborate marine decorations were in vogue. In majolica and barbotine wares, the decoration often overwhelmed the function, and the platters became objets d'art rather than practical eating implements. While most of the nineteenth-century affectations have disappeared from haute cuisine, much equipment associated with the enjoyment of fish has survived.

CHAPTER 8

liberation of libation

In dark cellars across the world fruits and grains have been fermenting for better and for worse since Creation. Wine, like the poor, we will always have with us, and there seems little new in the story of its popularity. There is something slightly novel, however, about the great display of ornament, rituals, and vessels crafted to accompany its enjoyment during the last three hundred years. If the period needs parentheses, two "new" potations came to encapsulate the social and decorative spectrum of imbibing. One was champagne, stylish and ever fashionable, as translucent and effervescent as the early eighteenth century when it made its debut. The other was absinthe — opaque, ornate, ornate, as phantasmagorical as the bistros favored by *fin de siècle* bohemians.

Without priests, how untoothsome our collective past would be. Since the lazy days along the prepharaonic Nile, they have not only taken on the monumental task of saving our immortal parts but tended to some very mortal needs as well. There is nothing like a well-run cloister for begetting transcendent notions of gastronomy.

While the grape was one of the earliest plants domesticated by humans, it was the clever, secretive, and serious priests of ancient Egypt who learned how to ferment grapes and preserve wine in clay jugs. Whether the ordinary pyramid-builder ever caught on to the process is difficult to say, because until recently only the powerful left records. But what evidence we have suggests it stayed a class secret.

The immodest Greeks, believing that anything good enough for gods was good enough for men, secularized wine making and made viticulture a popular and commercial success. Without them we might have been deprived of a lot of fun, a good deal of trouble, and a genre of fascinating objects that continues to entice collectors.

taste-vins

One of the most peculiar and compelling of these objects is the *taste-vin*, a small, shallow, saucerlike bowl, which sometimes has a dome-shaped bottom with fluted and engraved decorations on the side. Early ones appear to have had no handle, but later ones almost always did. This made using it a little more secure and provided a ring so it could be hung from a chain around the neck or on a belt.

It is impossible to say when the *taste-vin* was first stylized and widely used. Most certainly some implement for sampling has been around almost as long as connoisseurship itself, which is very old indeed. The ancient Romans produced some very credible vintages, and showed a marked preference for aged wines, which they imported from all over the Mediterranean. Horace left not only poems but records of his libations: "I had a jar of Alban over nine years old." A third-century fragment from the Oxyrhynchus Papyri of Greco-Roman Egypt mentions the professional wine taster but gives no clues to the tools of his trade.

By the late Middle Ages, French and German wines had begun to thrive and they crisscrossed Europe, becoming one of the first

major international businesses. While there are references as early as the fourteenth century to *taste-vins* in England and France, no actual objects survive. The sixteenth-century Flemish Calendar by Simon Bening in Munich's Bayerische Staatsbibliothek gives us one of the earliest hints of what the thing looked like. An illustration for the month October depicting transporting wine casts shows a wine merchant holding a taster, which is either wood or possibly ceramic. It is very close in design to the earliest surviving actual *taste-vin* in the British Museum, hallmarked 1601.

Wine classifications became more precise and geographically distinctive throughout the eighteenth century. Georgian England was practically afloat with wine; the demand was so great and the profits so easy that a huge amount of wine was adulterated or faked.

The Commandeur of a French chapter of the Confrérie des Chevaliers du Taste-vin was presented with this memento—worn on the end of a distinctive chain—of his office.

The handles of antique taste-vins are often crafted into serpent motifs, which evoke wine's connection with ancient myths and symbols. Snakes are emblematic of renewed youth and curative powers and are associated with the rites of Bacchus.

Educated tasting was crucial to successful buying and honest selling. It has been suggested that the silver *taste-vin* was invented by the wily French to fool the English by disguising the color and confusing the taste. Certainly transparent *taste-vins* would have been more revealing, and tasters made of glass were indeed used, as were ceramic and even wooden ones.

A likelier reason for the use of silver is that it was more durable and could withstand the rough treatment usual for early traveling wine merchants. A precious metal also conferred a hint of status.

The *taste-vin* briefly served another function. Referred to in early Louisiana inventories as *taste-indigos,* these were used to test the crystallization of indigo dye, that nastiest of cash crops. They are

Ancient Greeks might have used this glazed clay krater, or wine cup. Its design is a forerunner of later taste-vins. Examples survive made of faience, ceramic, and pewter. Vintners don't always agree whether tasters of silver or glass are best for gauging the true color of the wine.

identical to ones used for wine and were illustrated for that purpose by Diderot in his great eighteenth-century encyclopedia.

As the wine trade became more modernized, the *taste-vin* became largely decorative and its use ceremonial. It became the badge and weapon of many an intimidating sommelier. Particularly with the growth of wine societies and *confréries* toward the end of the nineteenth century, the *taste-vin* enjoyed a revival that was symbolic and decorative. The ones made today are used almost exclusively for this purpose, and unless they are associated with extraordinary persons or bear unusual inscriptions are of little interest. Eighteenth-century examples are highly desirable for the collector. Ceramic wine tasters, particularly English ones, are extremely rare, but nineteenth-century French faience tasters of great charm can still be found. Surviving glass tasters are generally not older than late nineteenth century, and the simplest appear to be the most authentic.

Few English tasters were made after 1800, but French ones are plentiful. Paris, Orléans, and Lyons were major centers for their fabrication. As a medium, silver allows wide latitude for decorative elaboration. In addition to the frequently used swirls and dimples which were worked into the sides to draw light into the liquid (and perhaps to identify which side one was sipping from), grapevines, fine chasing, and engraved names are often found on the body of the cup. Old coins were sometimes used in the bottoms of wine tasters as commemorations and decorations. One of the enigmatic motifs that frequently appear on *taste-vins* is a loop handle formed by a coiled serpent. Just as the shape of the cup suggested the design of ancient wine bowls, so this serpent decoration drew on primordial memory. The devotees of Dionysus, often called the god of wine, wound snakes around their arms during their bacchanalias. Snakes were symbols of renewed youth because they shed their skin. And the serpents that inhabited the temples of Ascelpius, the Greek healing divinity, were believed to be an antidote to illness and poison. The ouroboros, or serpent coiled swallowing its tail, had both cultic and alchemic significance, and classical silversmiths took the snake as their emblem. It is difficult to know how much of this was consciously understood by fabricators of *taste-vins*.

Taste-vins *were crafted to reflect personalized designs. Specialized shapes developed in major wine-growing regions in France, Germany, and Italy.*

coolers

From earliest times, people liked to mull wine, mixing it with everything from seawater to honey and herbs, drinking it hot and frothy. But who first thought to chill it and how this was done is a little secret no historian has sought to solve.

It is tantalizing to speculate on those heavy drinkers, the Romans. Evidence is still fragmentary about the equipment they used for cooling wine, but we know for certain it was done. Pliny the Elder, who rhapsodized over the tar-flavored wine from the French

town of Vienne (an early Côtes du Rhône), made a curious observation in his first-century work *Historia naturalis:* When this wine was served cold, it was colder than all others.

By the third century, people of taste certainly expected some good wine to be refrigerated. A travel log left by the Roman administrator Theophanes indicates that much of his journey from upper Egypt to Byblos (now Jubayl) in Lebanon was taken up in feeding his staff and himself. Reaching his destination, he splurged on some

Accounts of nineteenth-century households suggest wine coolers could also serve other things, like this late-eighteenth-century Irish cooler with sorbets.

The eighteenth-century carved wooden urn was made in Goa, India, for Western use.

The sideboard is set with nineteenth-century English champagne flutes, an Irish glass compote, and a tropically decorated Vieux Paris porcelain chilling tub, circa 1840.

Cellarettes were useful pieces of furniture in English and American dining rooms. This late-Georgian mahogany example could hold nearly a dozen bottles.

particularly expensive wine, as well as snow from the nearby mountains to cool it.

As heirs to all that was graceful in the classical world, the great monasteries of the Middle Ages took to the task of making wine and, if truth be told, drinking it. Where hauling snow was too tedious, streams, wells, and fountains were often employed for chilling purposes.

By the Renaissance, the preoccupation with wine was indisputable. Reception rooms were often overheated, and heavy clothing and heavier food created the desire for cold drink. Wine was kept cool in big tubs. Glasses were served on trays or were proffered by servants holding only the foot of a goblet and were quaffed in the same manner; the bowl of a drinking vessel was rarely touched.

A fifteenth-century allegorical engraving by Michael Wolgemut of King Solomon feasting depicts a basin with handles on paw feet. And by the end of the century material evidence of objects specifically designed as wine coolers begins to appear. An Italian majolica wine cistern dating from about 1550 is in the British Museum. Its oval shape that bellies out in the middle and then is pinched in above a wide foot was adopted as the standard form almost everywhere. These great basins seem to have been placed randomly near eating tables. Besides earthenware, they were often made of brass or marble and occasionally, for great personages, silver. Such cisterns were filled with iced water in which were floated large flagons or pitchers of wine and then later, by the early eighteenth century, batches of dark green bottles. It seems both red and white were enjoyed cold.

The earliest surviving English silver wine cistern is from around 1677, and there is a French one from a bit earlier. Certainly the grandest ever fabricated was the one executed by Charles Kandler of London in 1734 and now in the Hermitage, St. Petersburg. This magnificent creation supported by chained leopards and carved with classical motifs weighs almost 550 pounds. Cisterns in the later eighteenth century became more practical affairs, scaled down and placed on stands for convenience. Sometimes the metal basin was lavishly decorated with gilt and lacquer.

The growing sophistication of grape production in France and above all the "invention," that is to say the successful bottling, of champagne led to some stunning new equipment for presenting wine. The monteith, the *seau à bouteilles*, the *rafraîchissoir*, and the wine rinser were all a result of these developments. At once glamorous and practical, these beautiful methods of chilling individual bottles of wine and glasses at the table became de rigueur.

In England, cellarettes, enclosed boxes on legs, usually of mahogany and lined with lead or tin, were part of Georgian eating-room furniture and remained in vogue well into the nineteenth century. The appearance in France of a small table called a *rafraîchissoir* was the most graceful solution to keeping wine cool near the host's chair. The best examples have a marble top that was fitted with two metal-lined wells to hold iced bottles. It was usually also fitted with a shelf or two to hold glasses and plates.

While individual table wine coolers appeared timidly as early as the 1680s, none survive from before the first quarter of the eighteenth century. The English had a marked preference for silver "ice pails," as they were first called before the term "cooler" became common. With the invention of the rolled-plate process, often called Old Sheffield, great numbers of these were produced. Generally, they

The French impulse toward dining simply during the eighteenth century encouraged the creation of this rafraîchissoir, *a small serving table and wine cooler in one.*

The English excelled at silver wine coolers. With the invention of the rolled-plate process, decorative silver became more available. The Louis XV–period verrière *(right), used to chill wineglasses, is lacquered tole in the Chinese style.*

were sold in pairs and often in larger suites. There was a universal preference for the vase or krater shape, which was a conscious allusion to the ancient Greek origins of wine.

Beautiful French examples in silver exist as well. A fabulous pair of wine coolers made by the French silversmith Thomas Germain about 1727 as part of the Penthièvre-Orléans service of extraordinary French silver tableware were displayed at Versailles during an exhibition titled *The Royal Tables of Europe* in 1992–94. But table coolers found some of their most fanciful expression in porcelain and faience. The factories Sèvres, Meissen, and Worcester produced outstanding examples of porcelain table coolers. Even finely cut glass coolers were made, though they are rare. How, one wonders, did any survive the rigors of conviviality and the susceptibility of porcelain and glass to cracking if too cold?

The English were particularly fond of a multibottle cooler that had a crenelated edge called a monteith after a Scottish hero whose cape had a scalloped hem. This shape was adopted on the Continent as well because the crenellations were helpful for supporting bottle necks. Miniature versions of these to keep wineglasses chilled were called *verrières* or *seaux à verres* and were much used in France. The English and Americans had a marked preference for the individual wine rinsers at table. These were often cut crystal bowls with two small indentions on the lip to hold a stem and were used less to clean the glass than to refresh and cool it.

By the end of the eighteenth century, well-to-do households were well-stocked with wine-cooling paraphernalia. Their popularity continued until the end of the nineteenth century, when commercial manufacture of ice for household use and the introduction of mechanical cooling boxes rendered some of the older methods quaint. But the recent surge of interest in wine has revived not just admiration for these objects but the impulse to use them.

Highly decorated porcelain and ceramic tubs were popular for cooling wine. This English majolica piece is late nineteenth century.

drinking champagne

Is it possible to link the ample bosom of a queen to a scholarly, half-blind Benedictine monk and both to pleasures taken by three centuries of bons vivants without creating a *histoire scandaleuse?* Ah, perhaps not. Nevertheless it is precisely this delicious moral ambiguity wreathing the high style of champagne that has ensured its enduring popularity and has created interest in the lovely old paraphernalia that accompanies it.

Toasting any grand occasion, from a coronation to Gigi's debut at Maxim's, with anything but champagne would be unthinkable. The argument has never been whether to drink it, but how. In the dizzying spirals made by centuries of fashion, contemporary collectors are left with wide latitude for quenching their thirst in an aesthetically correct manner.

No doubt thinking of the graceful crystal flutes then popular, Madame de Pompadour once said champagne was the only wine a woman could drink without looking ugly. What would she have thought, one wonders, of that intimate photograph by Eugene J. Bellocq, the early-twentieth-century photographer who recorded the daily life of Storyville, the red-light district in New Orleans? Reclining among Turkish pillows, two ladies in camisoles awaiting gentleman callers sip Veuve Clicquot from something that looks suspiciously like soda fountain glasses!

Who actually invented champagne? The Romans knew the process of double fermentation to create a fizz, and the first-century poet Lucan describes how it was sealed in terra-cotta amphorae stored near cooling streams. That aside, it spoils the story not to imagine that all things began with Louis XIV's reign. Dom Pérignon, a monk who was nearly the exact contemporary of the Sun King, did perfect the cork and experimented further with encouraging an effervescence in the wines of his abbey during the second half of the seventeenth century. Not long afterward, champagne was brought to England. The charming and roguish French courtier Saint-Evremond passed some of his exile by teaching English royal circles to refine their table manners and enjoy this new sparkling wine. He insisted that the flute was the only proper way to enjoy champagne, and soon his friend, the Duke of Buckingham, had opened a factory

at Greenwich which produced flute-shaped vessels that set the style in England and America for almost two hundred years.

The early flutes were relatively short, with a bowl tapering either to a pointed or rounded bottom that rested on a stem often ornamented with a knop, or lump, which was sometimes faceted, sometimes not. The foot of the glass was often fairly large, it being generally felt that the foot, or base, should be about one-third larger than the diameter of the bowl for balance. Collectors who prize the evidence of that rough spot called a pontil mark on early blown glass might be interested to know that the folded foot, or base with a rolled edge, was a concession to the fine finishes on dining tables so a glass could slide without scratching. Later, of course, it became the rule to polish down the pontil to a smooth concave form, allowing the foot to rest flat on a surface.

The earliest examples of European flutes were made in the sixteenth-century glass factories of Venice. Always given to whimsy and improbability, Venetian artisans produced examples that stood on precarious stems, and were frequently decorated with gold tracery or colored jeweling. These flutes, which were probably inspired by the ancient glass of Byzantium, predate the popularity of champagne and were used for other wine. A painting by Velázquez, *Man with a Glass of Wine,* depicts a lovely flute gracefully held by the foot. What is in that glass we will never know, though it most certainly is not champagne. However, this shape became the inspiration for later glassmakers.

By the end of the eighteenth century, champagne drinking had spread from Monticello to Moscow. Czarina Catherine replaced Hungarian Toquay with champagne for official royal toasts, and a European commentator of the period remarked that in America a successful host was judged by the quantity and quality of his champagne. Yankees at that time preferred their champagne rose-colored and on the sweet side.

Everyone was using flutes for champagne. While the English flirted with air-twist decorations, those lovely spirals of white threads found in eighteenth-century glasses, and elaborate wheel engraving, elegant drinkers generally preferred simpler flutes clear enough to show the wine and remain steady in the hand after several refills. Usually the glass was paneled or ribbed and frequently the foot had cut decoration. Stems grew a little longer. In a painting by John Zoffany (1760), William Ferguson and friends are gathered around a mahogany tilt-top table under a large chestnut tree. They are celebrating with several bottles of champagne and drinking it from clever little flutes not unlike the ale glasses then in use. In a curious instance of reverse snobbery, the ale glass was often assertively distinguished from its aristocratic twin by the presence of an engraving of the hops plant along its rim.

The flute endured but did not go unchallenged. In a letter to his sister in 1832, the English dandy and later prime minister Benjamin Disraeli reported drinking champagne from a coupe. We may assume this was a novelty if it caught his somewhat precious eye. But the fashion for these saucer-shaped bowls on narrow stems took hold in the 1840s, and became ubiquitous on festive tables until about twenty-five years ago, when the flute staged a comeback.

The Venetians had crafted grand coupes (French for "cups") in the sixteenth and seventeenth century, but there is no evidence that they were used for champagne. English glassmakers produced a wide variety of similarly shaped objects, mainly used for serving sweetmeats and flummery. These glasses almost always had a rolled edge, which would have made them unsuitable as drinking vessels. It is not inconceivable that some creative hostess, wishing to be original, served her guests champagne in sweetmeat dishes and created a sensation, thus changing style.

A charming legend holds that Sèvres molded a milky-white porcelain coupe from the breast of Marie-Antoinette, giving us the origin of the shape. If history always imitated *art,* it would be far more amusing. Terrorists have nasty tongues, and the story may have been invented by a disgruntled antiroyalist, but there is a tantalizing coincidence that gives just a dash of truth to the tale. This backstairs gossip may have started at the little dairy Louis XVI built at Versailles to surprise his royal "milkmaid." The dairy was used as a refuge for Marie-Antoinette's private fetes, and Louis ordered a service of dishes in the most up-to-date style to be used for desserts.

Colored glass was developed very early in Venice. Later during the nineteenth century, Bohemian glass, much of it colored, was enormously popular throughout Europe and much imitated. This Louis Philippe period coupe is probably Baccarat circa 1850.

The form of glass coupes descends from the venerable ancestry of ancient goblets, but they were not used for sparkling wine until the end of the eighteenth century. The most charming explanation of this fashion is tied to the anatomy of a French queen. The middle glass is a mid-nineteenth-century compromise between the flute and saucer form.

Among the pieces commissioned at the Sèvres factory was a *jatte teton*, a breast-shaped cup with well-articulated nipple mounted on a tripod stand. The inspiration for this piece, whatever the proportions of the queen, was the Greek *mastos* cup, and Sèvres, knowing they had a good thing, continued to produce it into the nineteenth century.

Making the terrain of collecting more complicated, a compromise shape called the tulip appeared in the middle of the nineteenth century, but it had limited popular appeal. Partisans of each shape took to print, but it was on the tables of elegant houses that the battles were won and lost. Charles Tovey, writing a history of champagne in 1870, declared that "the old-fashioned tapering glass called a flute is the one generally preferred in champagne." But a 1903 photograph from the collection of the Museum of the City of New York shows a prenuptial party where the proper young bride-to-be is being toasted by her well-dressed friends with champagne in coupes. Given the Belle Epoque's love of the ornate, these coupes produced by fine glass companies such as Baccarat were richly cut and decorated.

Regardless of the shape of the glass, other equipment also evolved. While the nature of the champagne stopper did not require a corkscrew, something to loosen the foil and cut the wires was helpful, and corkscrews with these amenities proliferated. An imaginative English doctor, who prescribed a single glass of champagne a day for expectant mothers, invented a "tap" which penetrated the cork and allowed what remained in the bottle to keep its effervescence. Champagne has always been drunk a little warmer in Europe than America, but coolers and cellarettes were essential there as well. For the larger size of the champagne bottle, which the delicate or unsteady hand might mismanage, silver cradles were devised that assisted pouring.

Does a lovely glass or a handsome cooler improve the taste of champagne? That is a more profound philosophical question than can be solved here, but our senses are sociable and operate better in good company. The beautiful can only enhance the good, the desirable, and the tasty.

café society's stemware

Even if the French had no vineyards, they would have invented cafés. For who else could have so refined the art of sitting indoors and out, sipping drinks with the infinite leisure that is almost Zen? In 1720 the city of Paris alone had more than two hundred cafés, and scarcely a century later this number had reached four thousand. By

the Belle Epoque, even Gallic record-keeping could not account for how many such establishments existed in France. The word *boulevardier* was born on the wide, lively streets of nineteenth-century France, but the tendency perhaps originated in the older Roman habit of the plaza.

They could have sipped out of gourds or clay dishes, I suppose, but in fact chose glass. Between the late eighteenth century and the mid-twentieth century, Europeans and especially the French created an enormous quantity of marvelous chunky, irregular drinking glasses for everyday household and commercial use, with shapes and styles so various they defy categorization.

The tradition of glassmaking in France is an ancient one encouraged by the Romans. While a decline certainly occurred after the sixth century, by no means was the process wholly lost. The demand for window glass during the Gothic period and a market for luxury drinking glasses kept small factories going all over the country.

Opposite: Mid-nineteenth-century cut and faceted glass often imitated the more extravagant crystal models used in elegant households.

Below: These simple, straight-sided glasses, made with a heavy, irregular foot and varying height, are nineteenth-century commercial glass. Also from the nineteenth century, the hand-blown cider jug was a popular form in Normandy.

In the eleventh century, French glass masters helped establish at Altare, near Genoa, an extraordinary school of "gentleman" glassmakers, whose descendants five hundred years later revived glassworks from Flanders to Provence. It is true that by the eighteenth century, the standard for fine glass in Europe was being set first by the Venetians and then by glassmakers from Bohemia and England. But the French began catching up by the end of that century, and after the Revolution, Napoleon gave a huge impetus to the luxury trades in an effort to legitimize his empire. During this period the great houses of Baccarat, Saint-Louis, Clichy, and Le Creusot began producing stylish tableware again.

What has received almost no attention is the great quantity of commercial glassware produced independently throughout France during the nineteenth century to satisfy the burgeoning demand of ordinary households as well as restaurants and cafés. These glasses, despite technological advances, continued to have a handblown quality until the end of the century. Occasionally they were created to fill

Louis-Philippe period glasses are elegantly molded with cutwork to imitate details found in crystal glasses. Much more casual, tumblers or gobelets, called pastilles *because of the dimpled decoration, were favored in country settings to serve everything from lemonade to red wine. Appropriate for any number of occasions: the unadorned, short-stemmed glass and the dressed-up version with a fancy swirl at its base.*

a specialized regional need, such as cider and calvados in Normandy, or pastis in Provence, but much of this glassware seems to have been intentionally versatile. French glasses were made strong enough to hold everything from hot coffee to cold wine, balanced enough to withstand the shakiest hand, and thick enough to take a tumble or two without breaking.

The great appeal for a collector lies not in conventional elegance but eccentricity, not in a refined concept but in their rich, velvety feel. Held to the light, their rippled finish speaks of rollicking good times. The small ground dimple under the foot hints at some glassblower's hurried way of polishing off a product while his mind possibly strayed to the pleasures of its future contents. The one type of bistro glass which is easily identified is that used for absinthe.

Late eighteenth-century wine pitchers with crimped handles are graceful examples of the glassblower's art. Glass artisans also used decoration to disguise functions. In these glasses, the swirl design of the decoration served as a guide for measuring absinthe. This enormously popular drink among artistes and bon vivants was outlawed during the hysteria of World War I.

absinthe

Fairies, whether good or bad, are usually mischievous and always most troublesome company. *La fée verte*, or the Green Fairy, as absinthe was dubbed in the nineteenth century, was no exception. By the eve of the First World War, so much absinthe was being consumed in Europe and New Orleans that the late-afternoon time in the cafés was called *l'heure verte*, or the green hour — green because that was the liquor's hue before it was mixed with water, before it swirled into an opalescent cloud and the conviviality began, or the visions and nightmares descended. A concoction of herbs and alcohol, its crucial ingredient was a distillation of *Artemisia absinthium*, or wormwood.

Mentioned in ancient papyri, wormwood was used for various cures by the sophisticated Egyptians. Later the classical writer Pliny in his first-century work *Historia naturalis* recommended it for problems of the stomach and for worms, hence giving it the name. Science has confirmed that artemisia contains thujone, which does indeed stun roundworms, as well as brain cells, producing excitation, hallucinations, and even seizures in some people.

Wine laced with absinthe has been known since antiquity. Ancient Rome gave its victorious athletes a sip of the bitter-tasting mixture to remind them of reality amid their triumphs. Shakespeare's merry wives binged on purl, which was ale with a touch of absinthe. But absinthe wasn't really drunk on its own until the early nineteenth century. Around the 1790s some dotty maiden ladies called the Henriod sisters, living in the Val-de-Travers region of Switzerland bordering on France, gave a visiting dyspeptic Frenchman a sample of their homemade brew. Its secret ingredient was the *Artemisia absinthium* which grew wild in the area.

The herbal green absinthe, when mixed with water and sugar, swirls into an opalescent color. This powerful drink was charmingly referred to as la fée verte, *or the green fairy. Even after absinthe was banned, the taste for the licorice-flavored drink endured. As if to perpetuate the glory days of absinthe drinking, the old names have survived, even if they designate a less potent drink.*

This late-nineteenth-century nickel-plated spoon holder is a rare
bistro accessory, as are the graduated copper bistro bowls that
hold sugar cubes and sponges.

Absinthe glasses have a distinctive shape and were decorated in a
variety of ways. The etchings on these glasses, circa 1870, suggest
how high to pour the water.

The futuristic-looking Belle Epoque fountain announces the time
of the aperitif, which was traditionally from noon until 7 P.M.

The visitor, a Major Dubied, promptly fell under its spell, bought the recipe, and went into business with his son-in-law Henri-Louis Pernod to produce it. By 1805 the factory located in Pontarlier, France, was in full swing. A century later, dozens of factories would be operating there, making it the center of worldwide absinthe manufacture. Other names became famous, but Pernod remained the most recognized.

Without birds and soldiers, humans would rarely change their diets. Seeds and knapsacks have contained many enduring surprises. In the late 1840s, a functionary in King Louis-Philippe's war office decided that Pernod's "tonic" was just what men in uniform needed to fortify their spirits during the war in Algeria. By the end of that war the Pernod factory was producing twenty thousand liters a day, and returning soldiers had developed such a strong affection for the drink they were willing to pay when it was no longer part of rations.

Before long it was being served at every chic little café along the boulevards of Paris. Manet's startling canvas of 1859, *The Absinthe Drinker,* may have outraged staid Second Empire sensibilities, but it also served notice that the drink had come into its own. Its devotees included the most avant-garde painters and writers of the day. Degas, Gauguin, Toulouse-Lautrec, and Van Gogh depicted the drinking of absinthe in one form or another. Modigliani was inspired by the drink, and Picasso dedicated at least five canvases to the subject, as well as one bronze sculpture called *The Glass of Absinthe* (1914). Authors including Poe, Verlaine, and Rimbaud, drank absinthe and romanticized it in their writings.

Tots of absinthe would have been intoxicating enough, but they were usually accompanied by wines, cognacs, cigars, and titillating conversations. Who would not become dizzy or creative in such a milieu? *L'heure verte* was not just an interlude, it was a way of life. And the growing public condemnation of absinthe by the forces of propriety and health made it all the more delicious to the bohemian set. For the delicate, the susceptible, or the addicted, it could be dangerous, even fatal. There seems little doubt it played a crucial part in the sad finish of both Van Gogh and Toulouse-Lautrec.

However much our virtues have forsaken rituals, our vices at least still thrive on them. The ceremony and paraphernalia of absinthe drinking were and remain among its great attractions. Absinthe was served in a tall glass; across its mouth a slotted spoon was placed to hold a lump of sugar, over which water was poured. The drink, thus sweetened, was stirred, giving it an alluring opalescence.

Although absinthe was banned everywhere except Spain and England in 1915, the laws were not stringently enforced, and many of the accoutrements have survived. Glasses came in many designs, often marked by some form of decoration or etched line to suggest how much to pour. If the variety of absinthe spoons is any indication, this drink engendered as much delight in the implements as the consumption. There were at least 125 different designs for slotted spoons, including models using intricately worked names, depictions of the Eiffel Tower, and various leaf, star, and cross motifs. Labels and advertising posters called forth some of the best graphic designs of the period, full of the swirls and flourishes of Art Nouveau. Carafes, match strikes, and Jules Verne–looking fountains that now fetch huge prices were part of every café's repertoire. Our own fin-de-siècle fascination with the decadence and mystery of absinthe has created a great demand for the decorative works of *la fée verte,* who may be in hiding but has not disappeared.

An example of the poster designs from the Art Nouveau period, French artist Privat Livemont's 1898 lithograph uses ethereal imagery to advertise the hallucinogenic green liquor.

*l*andscaping the *d*ining room

In sheparding the culinary arts to near perfection during the last three centuries, the French also touched off a decorative volcano that has spewed out every sort of implement and accoutrement for the preparation and elegant consumption of food. Fine porcelain and glassware, silver implements and serving pieces came with all due dispatch to the French tastemakers and were transmitted promptly to the rest of the hungry Amero-European world. But for some reason it only slowly dawned on the French that a specific room in which to eat all these elaborate victuals and a permanent surface on which to serve them were desirable.

In France and elsewhere on the Continent, the trestle table endured as the preferred type of table for dining until the end of the eighteenth century. This eighteenth-century Spanish colonial table is made of sabino wood.

the table

A fresco at Monte Oliveto, Sienna, by Giovanni Sodoma (1508) gives a rare glimpse at an early set dining table. The table, certainly used for many other purposes, is set for six, with rather artistic touches. The narrow benches, standard seating until the end of the Renaissance, seemed comfortable for both artisan and archduke.

The English, poor dears, until lately have not been known for stirring pots to a most savory finish. But they must at least be credited for originating one significant element of modern gastronomic life: the dining table. By the time Louis XV was commissioning what seemed like the novel idea of a private dining room in Versailles, many a country gentleman across the Channel was quite used to eating regularly in a special room. Their Gallic counterparts were still folding up simple wooden trestles with unfinished removable tops and storing them in armoires as late as Marie-Antoinette's day.

The ancients practiced the custom of dining formally. By the time Vitruvius wrote *On Architecture* at the end of the first century B.C., the *triclinium,* or dining room, was a well-established feature of all comfortable patrician houses. Both literary descriptions and archaeological evidence make it clear that the Romans took the ritual and hospitality of dining seriously. During the Republic, men lay on couches while they ate; respectable women took meals sitting on stools or chairs. Later all reclined in the *triclinium;* the traditional arrangement of three large couches each holding three persons arranged in a semicircle around low marble or bronze tables gave the room its Latin name. A sense of the lavish decoration of these rooms is suggested by the mosaics in the Villa of the Falconer at Argos in Greece and in the pavements of Volubilis. By the late-Roman period, couches were placed like spokes around circular tables. Diners supported themselves on the left elbow, using only the right hand to eat. Later, as the empire collapsed, reclining went out of fashion.

A millennium later, the medieval privileged classes lived quite differently. Their houses were first and foremost fortresses, not villas, and their lives exceedingly peripatetic. Furniture was sparse and movable. Dining took place either intimately before a bedroom fire or publicly in some great state hall. Tables were thrown up by placing long boards covered with neatly folded linen cloths on sawhorse-like trestles. Likely as not, the benches brought out to line one side of the table served other purposes as well. Meanwhile, peasants, out of convenience, gathered to eat around the kitchen work table routinely.

Even when benches gave way to chairs in the fifteenth century, tables were rarely important. In paintings depicting eating scenes throughout the late Middle Ages and Renaissance, there are always makeshift tables or small center tables that can be detected under the long skirts. The one exception could be found in that bastion of security and cultural continuity, the monastery. Noble houses came and went; the fortunes of war might sweep away knight, castle, and rich merchant, but the great abbeys endured. Their refectories were central gathering places, and their dining tables were usually permanent affairs. In the religious upheaval of the sixteenth century, apostasy brought profits to the English gentry. The rich land and even richer buildings and goods of the monastic orders became the property of ambitious courtiers. A lord who laid claim to some well-appointed

The French farm table, such as this late-eighteenth-century Provençal walnut example, answered all sorts of kitchen needs, among them a place to eat.

A French walnut Jacob-style dining table, circa 1800, features nine leaves. By the beginning of the nineteenth century, the dining table was an essential and unique piece of furniture.

Estate inventories show that valuable dining tables by skilled cabinetmakers were rare in France before 1770. The introduction of an expanding table with a mechanism for runners to accommodate multiple leaves swept the fashionable classes in the period of Louis XVI.

abbey was hardly likely to turn the dining hall into a stable or chop a costly refectory table into kindling.

Heavy rectangular joined tables on baluster legs became increasingly identified as dining tables in England. The incorporation of a concealed draw leaf that could extend its length, probably an Italian idea, added to their versatility. Tables such as these are still called *tables Italiennes* in France. With this began the slow development of "mechanical" innovations that allowed tables to expand and contract. The gate-leg and drop-leaf tables popular in Holland were also widely used in England in the seventeenth century and provided a measure of the old idea of flexibility in dining arrangements. Samuel Pepys in the 1660s praised his new "dining table" which could seat eight comfortably but ten also very well. Later he extolled the oval table introduced by Sir Philip Warwick which could be opened to accept leaves when unexpected visitors arrived.

It was a hundred years before such tables became known, much less adopted, in France. References to French dining rooms are scarce before the middle of the eighteenth century. Engravings depicting dinners other than grand ones of state show them occurring in rooms with beds or in cozy sitting rooms. Rarely is a piece of furniture specifically called a dining table mentioned in official inventories. If they do appear in those appraising documents, the value ascribed is minimal, indicating they were not the work of the important cabinetmakers. Madame de Pompadour had made for her Paris establishment a table of good wood that could accommodate leaves. Likely she got the idea from Stanislaw Leszczyński, high-living king of Poland, who supposedly had the first such table at his chateau in Lorraine. It was not until the last quarter of the eighteenth century

Before the middle of the eighteenth century, most private meals were taken on small occasional tables such as this provincial Louis XV walnut table. Such tables were also used for writing, working, or other pursuits.

that famous cabinetmakers like J.-P. Reboul made a specialty of a mechanical six-legged table that as an oval could seat a few people but had a system of runners that would pull out to accommodate leaf after leaf. The largest of these could seat more than thirty, although most were built for twelve to fourteen. These quickly became part of the patrician household.

By the end of the nineteenth century, a special table and room to dine in became fundamental to social respectability. Furniture styles grew heavier and more ostentatious as the middle classes became more powerful and less relaxed. The vast surfaces were designed to hold the substantial cuisine of the period as well as an array of porcelain, silver, and ornament. The dining table's topography became both a training ground and social battlefield.

The English pioneered fine permanent dining tables, and the Americans followed suit. This two-part dining table was crafted of Santo Domingan mahogany in the early nineteenth century in Baltimore.

fingers to forks

Well before the notion of a discrete room or special table had been widely established, specific implements had begun to be adopted across Europe as essential for dignified dining. But it is obvious that wielding tools other than one's fingers while eating does not come naturally to *Homo famelicus,* and the process has been vexing. Take, for example, the tortured history of the fork.

By modern standards, early feasts were sloppy affairs, without napkins, porcelain plates, or forks provided by the host. A sensible dinner guest brought his own fork. This late-sixteenth-century steel and walnut two-pronged implement was an early form of the fork.

The popular thread-and-shell pattern, first introduced in the eighteenth century, continues to adorn fashionable tables in America, England, and France.

Prior to the 1860s, knives were rarely manufactured en suite with forks and spoons. This Georgian spinach-dyed ivory set with silver mounts, circa 1790, is a notable exception.

In the late nineteenth century, Gorham made these macabre pieces adorned with pantherlike creatures in the delightfully surprising Bar pattern, paying homage to the large European pieces. From the Marsh Collection, Pittsburgh, Pennsylvania.

Opposite, top: *French standards for silver have always been high. French first standard has a slightly higher silver content than that of English or American sterling.*

The marvelous thing about predicting the worst is that one is rarely wrong. So when a young Byzantine bride met an early end in eleventh-century Venice, the high clergy and elders were not surprised — for she had introduced a small golden pronged thing for eating at supper parties, an affectation they had promptly denounced as degenerate and dangerous. Even sweet St. Peter Damian, ever vigilant against worldliness, was sufficiently exercised to point a finger at the innovation. After all, it is not the thing a hermit would find appealing. These jeremiads were just the kind of recommendation irresistible to fashionable people of any age.

The spoon, an abstraction of a cupped hand, and the knife, perhaps an extension of a long tooth, have been in use since the Bronze Age. Although a tantalizing illustration survives from a 1023 edition of Hrabanus Maurus's *Glossaria* depicting two gentlemen eating meat with forks, the glamorous medieval table was set with trenchers of hard-baked bread and no implements, unless perhaps a long flat knife. Little forklike tridents were used for picking up the gooey can-

Left: Soigné dinners required a hostess to provide every utensil imaginable for her guests' convenience. Standing chests housed an army of silver, such as this extraordinary 363-piece set by Tiffany in the Kings pattern.

These alligator-pattern forks and spoons by New Orleans silversmith Ellis Joubert recall a popular souvenir pattern of the early twentieth century.

The culinary panoply, from flatware to salt and pepper shakers, was miniaturized for children, from infancy through adolescence.

Leading manufacturers produced a variety of youth sets, including Chantilly and Lily of the Valley by Gorham and a knife and fork by Georg Jensen.

died fruit called sucket, but for some reason they had not been adapted for general eating. Gradually the use of the fork came to be viewed as the only acceptable way to convey solid food to the mouth. The practice spread slowly through Italy to France and the Low Countries until it reached England in the seventeenth century. Despite notable royal holdouts like Louis XIV and Queen Anne, who preferred to use their fingers rather than manipulate the foolish fork, it was reluctantly adopted even by sensible sorts by the end of that century. With its introduction, the stage, or should we say the table, was set for the development of elaborate flatware.

It had been the habit until the end of the sixteenth century for guests to bring their own cutlery to dinner parties — an awkward but sanitary expedient. But soon new customs, cuisines and etiquettes ensured the fork's place on the table. Where the custom of carrying "personal" cutlery survived, it was usually reserved for instances of traveling. By the end of the seventeenth century the proper table began to be regularly set by the host. With the appearance of the new French "international" cuisine in the eighteenth century and the adoption of a complicated way of serving called French service, the need for laying down table utensils for each place became imperative and sets of flatware became desirable.

In the late eighteenth and early nineteenth centuries, complete child-size tea sets, such as this Vieux Paris pattern, circa 1850, were used to instill an early appreciation for the delights of the table. Dinner sets, including compotes, tureens, sauceboats, and platters, taught the complexities of dining with adults.

Blade design can be a clue to a table knife's age. The spearlike point gave way to a hlunter shape in the eighteenth century.

"Flatware" is actually a much later American term, coined to distinguish the relatively solid fork and spoon from "hollow ware," which meant vessels such as teapots and ewers. Everywhere except in America until quite recently, these articles were referred to simply as table spoons and table forks because they belonged to the table rather than the person. Today this term creates confusion because a table spoon or fork is usually associated with serving pieces. Compared to much modern-day silver, the old place forks and spoons do seem large in scale. Other pieces were usually identified by their function, such as teaspoons, dessert forks and spoons, and fish eaters. In early sets, serving implements were almost always separate and of different design. Old table knives were originally steel, and had ivory, bone, horn, wooden, or, less commonly, silver handles. Until the end of the nineteenth century they were rarely included in large flatware services as matching pieces.

A marking system for silver began in the fourteenth century, although a separate indication for the date appeared much later and in some places not at all. The earliest dated silver fork in the collections of the Victoria and Albert Museum bears a mark of London, 1632. Silver marks became a means of guaranteeing the quality of the metal as well as the workmanship. Learning the marking system for each country is a study in itself. The most fundamental distinctions are the terms that express degrees of fineness or purity of worked silver. The French came to employ the term "first standard," which indicated that the object was 95 percent pure, reserving a "second standard" for things less pure, less fine, but often stronger. "Second standard" is roughly equivalent to the American designation "coin silver," which was not necessarily made from coins but referred to a silver content around 90 percent. The most familiar is a standard called "sterling," which both the English and Americans adopted, representing articles that were 92.5 percent pure silver.

From the middle of the eighteenth century, quantities of silver tableware were made, much of which survives today. The introduction of a silver-plating process adaptable to large-scale flatware manufacturing by the French firm Christofle was quickly mimicked in England and America, making this amenity available to even more people. Services of flatware became de rigueur for all respectable households, and indeed until quite recently social status was most clearly indicated by the quality and completeness of a family's cutlery.

Certain basic silver patterns endured through the late nineteenth century. In France the most popular were the *uniplat,* a simple design much like the Hanoverian silver in England, and the *filet,* or "fiddle thread." Variations developed by adding a "rat tail" or fashioning a "dog nose," feathering an edge, or adding a shell. In Europe as well as America, versions of these forms were produced in great numbers. A service in which all the pieces were made by the same person or workshop at the same time is much rarer before 1850. By the 1870s, the application of steam machinery transformed the manufacture of silver tableware. The patenting of pattern designs in the United States began a virtual avalanche of styles in the late nineteenth century. For some collectors, the charm of unmatched sets has retained a special appeal.

Another arena of flatware collecting is miniature children's flatware. We know that the European delight in "baby houses" — created by some of the great craftsmen of northern Europe — became particularly strong in the seventeenth century and that they were essentially an expensive pastime for adults.

But by the late nineteenth century, dollhouses had become largely the domain of children. There is a marvelous range of utilitarian objects that were scaled down to make them more manageable for children. These were devised as toys but were meant to be an "improving" amusement, with socialization as the goal. Using such elegant equipage helped to widen children's knowledge of respectable domestic routines. In wood, silver, and ceramic, these pieces continue to compel collectors.

traveling in style

Roaming to eat is a habit humankind seems disinclined to resist. This must be rooted in the primeval experience of hunters who wandered any distance to bag some toothsome prey. What crude implements our tribal ancestors used for these nomadic repasts is unclear. Bare hands are useful and so are any sharp and pointed objects, as most modern travelers know too well. The resumption of widespread travel after the seventeenth century, the lingering medieval tradition of personal cutlery, and the notion that refined table equipment was an index to status produced the fashion for lavish traveling sets.

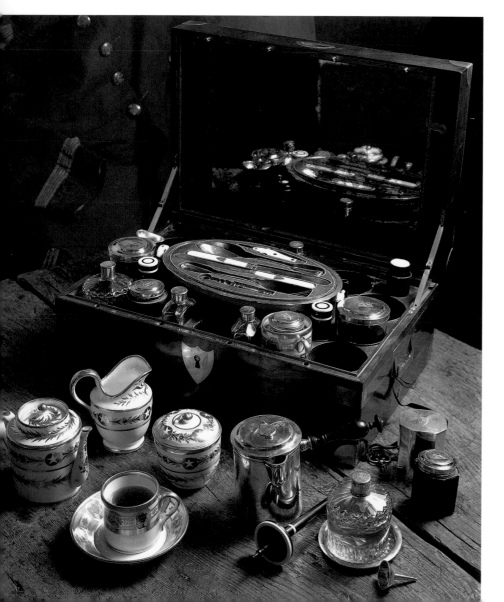

Folding knives had been known since Roman days, but the cause of personal cutlery was greatly advanced by the invention of the back spring, which allowed for clever folding devices for small forks and knives. Elaborate versions with handles of pearl, ivory, ebony, or semiprecious stone and blades and tines of silver or steel survive from the seventeenth and eighteenth centuries. Sometimes the ends of the implement were threaded, enabling them to be unscrewed from the handle. Sets were cunningly fitted into cylinders of wood carved with shaped compartments and lined with chamois.

Often called nécessaires de voyage, *extravagant boxes like this one made in 1791 for the French Revolution leader Nicolas de Barras provided for more than simple needs. It contains fifty pieces: various eating utensils, sewing implements, and a portable writing desk with secret compartments. The encased ruler suggests its owner might be at work on military maps while taking his meal.*

An example of luxurious ingenuity, the portable silver tea set includes pots that fit inside one another for economical packing. It also has equipment to boil water. Such sets were in much demand by members of the Austro-Hungarian nobility, who had vast distances to travel in that far-flung empire. This set was made around 1830.

These were fitted into a silver or gold beaker, which was slipped into a carrying case, usually of richly dyed morocco.

Although variations on these kits were made into the twentieth century, the heyday of their design was between 1760 and 1860. The use of precious metals and the frequent presence of armorial devices leave little doubt as to the clientele for these objects. About 1710 the German silversmith Paul Solanier of Augsburg equipped a handsome octagonal case with bowl, plate, spice box, fork, soup spoon, and teaspoon. Indeed, the demand for ever more luxurious sets led to the inclusion of all sorts of miscellaneous items, including toilet articles. The most sumptuous traveling ensemble in the eighteenth century was probably the multipiece set created for Marie-Antoinette by Jean-Pierre Charpenat. In addition to silver and porcelain eating

A traveler in the Orient might have needed this shagreen-cased trousse, or traveling kit, with chopsticks, knife, and ivory tongue cleaner.

Culinary tools were also stored within compartments of canes, made since the fifteenth century. These nineteenth-century models carry chopsticks, a corkscrew, and nutmeg graters. Louis XIII had one that held a candy box.

This Charles X period traveling decanter set with matching goblets, probably Saint-Louis crystal, is circa 1820.

The neatly organized vermeil and mother-of-pearl traveling set was made in France during the First Empire. Designed for several meals, it would have been carried for travel by horse-drawn coach.

implements and various tea and chocolate pots, it held an ivory-handled mirror, perfume flagons, sewing implements, and a bed-warming pan.

By the nineteenth century, travel had become a vastly popular pastime among all the respectable classes. The standard in sets was established by the French silversmith Martin-Guillaume Biennais. Gossip had it that the first of his extravagant sets made for Napoleon was delivered on credit before the Egyptian campaign. The general, ever grateful for this show of confidence, made him famous and successful during the Empire. The traveling sets Biennais designed often comprised thirty or forty pieces fitted into boxes the size of small trunks.

Less elaborate sets continued being made into the twentieth century for specialized needs such as colonial travel, safaris, and even picnics. But travelers' needs were increasingly being catered to by modern transportation. The Packet service instigated by the American Black Ball Lines in the early nineteenth century set a lavish standard for service which was adopted by European counterparts. While contemporary literary travelogues still urged tourists to bring along their own cutlery and even pots and pans, by midcentury the introduction of rapid and dependable passenger trains and the incorporation of food service aboard most of them transformed the need for and hence the content of traveling sets. Gradually the cosmetic replaced the culinary, and the pocket folding knife and fork became a quaint reference to earlier times.

Wars could be inconvenient, but the gentleman officer carried certain amenities with him. This eighteenth-century English mahogany traveling military case contains decanters, glasses, and wine funnels.

More modest traveling sets for the pocket only sometimes had a glass, though the leather cases always offered folding implements. The Georgian apple-corer was meant to fit a vest pocket.

napery

From the earliest times, textiles were among the most prized, protected, and passed down of treasures. Wherever humankind settled and had time to make something lovely, we find the remains of cloth. Table linens are no modern innovation; they were in fact almost the first refinement of epicureans.

Cotton weaving in ancient Egypt was nothing short of fabulous. Three thousand years before the Christian era, the Egyptians were able to produce cotton cloth so fine we can count almost twice the number of threads per inch than our best cloth has today. No wonder the Egyptian weaver claimed descent from the goddess Isis. Genesis and Confucius, Homer and Herodotus all extolled the qualities of good cloth.

In ancient Rome there was a brief vogue for *mappae,* large handkerchief-napkins embroidered in gold. Diners in Rome had the custom of bringing their own large napkin to banquets. It served as both bib and towel and at supper's end to bag up leftovers to take home.

It was really not until the Middle Ages that the use of tablecloths became widespread, and it might be argued that the decoration of castle tables mimicked that of cathedral altars. Early European paintings show that the trestle table was either covered with artfully ironed great cloths or long runners laid side by side. With the appearance of the "dining table" and "dining room," this style of runner went out of fashion, only to be revived at the end of the nineteenth century as "refectory sets," comprising two runners, two place mats, and a centerpiece.

By the end of the Renaissance the great textile centers of Europe were well established. Although light embroidery on mesh had been done for some time, it cannot be confused with actual lace, which is only about 350 years old. A collector's pilgrimage evokes a grand tour of place names: *point de Venise* and Genoa velvet in Italy, Honiton lace in England, Brussels lace, and Irish linen. Nowhere was the textile industry more vibrant than in France. Few kings were as fond of lace as the grand Louis XIV. His clever minister Colbert encouraged its manufacture, and all over France, place names stand for quality lace and cloth.

The capacious shelves of the linen press stored the vast needs of a household for napkins and table linens. Linens that were not in daily use were frequently wrapped in blue paper to avoid yellowing.

The delicate patchwork of fine laces handmade between 1900 and 1920 often has an ethereal quality. The piece shown combines examples of Normandy, Valenciennes embroidery on net, Brussels, and Limerick.

Scrolling white embroidery can complement additional designs and borders of realistic forget-me-nots, filet lace inserts, Cluny lace edging, and point de Venise.

By the end of the eighteenth century there were looms clacking all over colonized America as well. Early attempts to establish a silk and linen industry in the South met with disappointing results, and the most successful commercial efforts occurred in the Northeast. It would be a mistake to imagine that the palette of the past was tastefully white and simple. Wherever technology allowed, color and intricate design were incorporated. Even domestic "homespun" displayed vivid and imaginative decoration.

The seventeenth and eighteenth centuries saw the tablecloth emerge as an essential article for the fashionable house. Like silverware, table linens measured a family's wealth. They begin appearing in American house inventories quite early. In 1640 James Olmstead of Wethersfield, Connecticut, who lived in a modest two-room cottage, was recorded as having "two tablecloths and four napkins." The account of nosy Jean-Baptiste Garic, notary of New Orleans, is more telling. Appraising the possessions of one recently deceased

citizen in July of 1769, he lists the contents of the dining room, including 22 tablecloths and 200 napkins, of which, he hatefully remarks, 158 are soiled.

Napkins had been used by the French court since the fifteenth century, and had been recommended to refined sensibilities by every etiquette manual since Erasmus, but people still resisted them. No less a personage than George Washington, in his little book of the 1750s, *The Rules of Civility*, urged his contemporaries to refrain from using the tablecloth to clean their face. In fact, that was exactly what many were doing with the edges of the ample tablecloths that draped across their laps. Foreign observers a century later were still appalled by the same habits.

The size of napkins waxed and waned. Early ones were often long stretches of cloth that could service a whole line of guests. By the eighteenth century, napkins had become individual and enormous but did not necessarily match the tablecloth. The fashion for

The drudgery of washing and ironing was necessary to properly maintain the table linens of every family. Soot and scorching could turn the task of laundering from triumph to tragedy.

Laundry marks could be made up of simple initials or possess a more elaborate design to commemorate a marriage or title. Some of these marks even helped the mistress of the household maintain the inventory of her supply.

matching table linen and the "lapkin" after the 1840s carried on this tradition of huge squares of linen sometimes three feet across to protect the ample figures and flounces of diners. By the end of the century, napkins began to shrink; by the 1920s they had assumed the miserable dimensions popular in the present, when they finally turned to paper.

The boom period for table coverings, doilies, and napkins began in the prosperous years after the middle of the nineteenth century. The introduction of the Jacquard loom in 1851 and other innovations allowed cloth to be woven in full widths and various patterns. The mechanization of the textile industry meant that a large supply of high-quality linen and cotton was being produced. When new processes were finally applied to lace making, machine-made lace was actually preferred over handmade, not just because it was cheaper but because it was thought of as better. It meant that a much larger public could own and use highly decorated table linens. In America, most quality damask was still imported from Ireland, France, and Belgium, but was often finished here with fine embroidery, appliqué, or lace. Few hope chests of even the poor did not contain some table linens. Well into the twentieth century, proper young women learned the skills of a beautifully hand-turned hem, intricate drawn work, and hemstitching. Perhaps some of the finest work of this sort came out of convents and orphanages, where patience and aesthetics formed part of the discipline.

Linens have always been prized and will be as long as there is an imagination left to be caught in the warp and weft of finely placed threads. For centuries, well-pressed, well-hemmed table coverings and accessories have been a sign of good housekeeping, good taste, and good sense. Spreading a freshly laundered cloth, folding an extravagantly large "lapkin"— these gestures tell us of enduring values and profound pleasures.

Tape lace forms a chrysanthemum pattern in an extremely fine centerpiece, circa 1900. Its bold design ensured that it would not be overshadowed by the profusion of cut glass and silverware.

Lord Penrhyn ordered an exquisite suite of table linens for the 1886 visit of Queen Victoria to Penrhyn Castle. Woven into the damask was his coronet, cipher, and family crest. The development of the Jacquard loom facilitated special orders with personalized designs, but they still remained exceedingly expensive.

Potage Bisque
Filets de Saumon Brésilienne
Jambon d'Yorck, sauce Madère
Canetons rôtis Rouennais
Surprises de foies gras
Salade vénitienne
Corbeilles de fruits
Coulommier
Glace au café et à la vanille
Fours et Fruits glacés

*m*enu as *m*anifesto

If the cookbook begins this story, the menu provides a convenient leaving-off place. With its appearance, one thing is certain: all elements have come together to create the dining rituals we still vaguely recognize today. Table and chair, room and routine, fork and finery had met and merged in the well-turned-out dining experience by the nineteenth century. New technologies made it possible to reach the heights and depths of extravagance, new foods and new dishes redefined grand cuisine, and tabletop equipment expanded like the volume of a soufflé in an oven. Perhaps most importantly, new culinary personalities had emerged. The appearance of the chef as celebrity and the gourmand as critic was indispensable for completing this epicurean epic.

By the end of the eighteenth century, the increasing number of widely distributed cookbooks were no longer content merely to list recipes; they began to sketch out programs for whole meals. Although earlier examples survive, such as Bartolomeo Scappi's detailed accounts of papal meals in his *Cooking Secrets of Pope Pius V* (Venice, 1570), these were not quite in the same spirit of those that appeared later. Chefs may have been interested in set menus and followed them, but it was not thought particularly important that guests know what they were eating. It was sufficient simply to amaze them. In the first century, Petronius, whose satirical *Satyricon* must have struck some true chords, described in the section of that work titled "Trimalchio's Feast" a dinner party where guests were entertained by a huge wooden hen laying eggs made of pastry.

This passion for visual spectacle rather than gustatory satisfaction survived at the medieval table, where heralds sometimes trumpeted the entry of a dramatic but foul-tasting dish. Despite the fact that China had the most developed cuisine of that time, when Marco Polo described dining with the Great Khan he was more interested in telling how the table reflected power and anthropological differences than in dwelling on more savory aspects.

To be sure, there had been famous cooks before, but by the end of the seventeenth century, chefs were becoming celebrities, and a well-laid table became the aspiration of every host and hostess. The suicide of François Vatel, head of kitchens for the Prince de Condé, in 1671 can give a sense of the pressures felt by fastidious chefs. Vatel locked himself in his room and fell upon his own knife, disgraced by the failure of provisions to arrive for a lunch in honor of Louis XIV.

In the ensuing century, kings and intellectuals aspired to become amateur cooks and vied to create new dishes, which were named not for their ingredients but after fashionable people. Sauces told more about society than cotillions did. In the eighteenth century, concoctions named Richelieu, Soubise, Mornay, and Du Barry became fundamental to the new cooking. Later it was preparations called Rothschild and Rockefeller that crowned mutton or oysters, and finally food embraced the demimonde of entertainment. Singers

Page 166 and opposite: French was the international culinary language for more than two hundred years. No one who could not decipher a French menu could be considered a serious gourmet. This Art Nouveau menu is held by a rococo-style silver menu holder, circa 1900.

Given the complexity of nineteenth-century banquets, it was thought wise to alert guests as to what was to come. The menu became both a program and a caution, lest a guest be tempted to overeat early in the meal. These Baccarat crystal and silver holders are early twentieth century.

and actresses like Nellie Melba and Sarah Bernhardt conferred their fame on creations from equally famous kitchens. Menus served as a social column as much as an outline of the night's event.

Perhaps the earliest table menu meant to be inspected by guests is one found in the Library of the City of Paris, dating from the marriage of the Dauphin and Marie Josephe de Saxe in 1747. At the same time, a popular cookbook, *La Cuisinière bourgeoise*, appeared, promising the "public" that they too could eat like princes. It was here that *menu* was first defined as "a paper on which is written the name of all that will be served at a dinner."

Place-card holders, such as these French Belle Epoque cherubs, seem certainly to have evolved from menu holders.

Edwardian menu holders are set off by the Duchess of Windsor's menu request and a note regarding a dinner she would later attend.

It wasn't only at fancy dinner parties that menus were expected; by the twentieth century they had become ubiquitous. This 1930 English brass holder was part of the Royal Ordnance officer's mess paraphernalia.

Finally, it is with the more than sixty watercolor menus from 1751 and 1757 by Brain de Sainte-Marie that we recognize the true ancestor of the modern menu. Drawn up for the intimate dinners given by Louis XV and La Pompadour for sixteen to twenty friends, they were meant as a guide to the evening — assuming that the guests wanted to know what they were eating and what to anticipate. The evocative-sounding "new cuisine" created a new language that was to sweep Europe and America and dominate the food scene for more than two and a half centuries. Menus in the ensuing years might become shorter and the decoration less precious, but the lan-

These English sterling silver holders are quite heavy and were probably intended for yacht use.

guage stayed French. Menus, no longer a rarity, became expected for any formal meal.

Their other significance was a tacit recognition of the presence at table of a new personality: the informed gourmand who knew food, took it seriously, and expected complexity, competence, and creativity at the table. The gourmand began as a character, sometimes aristocratic, sometimes intellectual, in rather elite eating clubs or at society tables. Gradually in France this type became increasingly democratized. In the bourgeois culture after the Revolution, an almost rabid desire to be respectable, coupled with the more broadly

Exoticism was a powerful ingredient in late-nineteenth-century art and style, and just as Monet fell under the sway of Japanese taste, so did hosts and hostesses in Europe and America. The bronze doré holders are circa 1890. The menu is from the same period.

distributed industrial wealth, produced an atmosphere of culinary striving. Chefs in private houses and in the new public restaurants responded to the new demands for excellence and reciprocally raised the bar of judgment among their clientele.

The emergence of the restaurant was of course a vital step in the development of the written menu. This type of establishment, which we now take for granted, probably emerged around the 1760s. By the early years of the nineteenth century there were over four thousand restaurants in Paris alone. Gourmands such as Brillat-Savarin and Grimod de la Reynière wrote treatises on the philosophy of food, and sophisticated gluttony became a mark of distinction. Amateur food critics and self-conscious gastronomic eating clubs were springing up all over Europe.

It is possible to recognize dishes and ingredients on early menus, but ultimately these documents appear almost incomprehensible because of their structure. Until the middle of the nineteenth century, fancy dining followed the arcane procedures of French service. Essentially what distinguished French service was the presentation of many dishes on the table at one time. Not exactly organized in courses as we know them today, these removes would be placed on the table in complicated geometric patterns at one time by an army of servants, who were supported by battalions of cooks. Each remove might include meats and vegetables, even sweets and savories. Guests' plates were passed around the table to be filled from the nearest tureen or platter. The enormous number of serving pieces in a dinnerware set is evidence of the requirements of French service. The *relèves* generally included soups, entrées, *rôtis,* and desserts. As each course was removed and the new course laid, the strict geometry of the table was preserved. It was what we have come to think of as a "family style" table pyramided with dozens of selections. However inconvenient or however unlikely it was that a guest would get the desired morsel or get it hot, no one could argue against the sheer culinary magnificence of this presentation.

By the nineteenth century, advocates of simpler domestic arrangements, hot food, and fewer servants adopted Russian service. Meat was carved and placed on the plates, platters were passed to guests rather than plates moving across a riotous table, and courses as we know them became more rigidly defined.

As the French invention of *"grande cuisine"* became ever more grandiose under chefs like Carême and Escoffier during the nineteenth century, it came to dominate fashionable circles from St. Petersburg to Pittsburgh. The diaspora of chefs from France carried recipes and styles everywhere they went. Fashionable people and comfortable householders prided themselves on a repertoire of fancy food that emulated these standards. Its intricacies relied heavily on the new international codes that were encrypted in menus, and their comprehension set the cognoscenti apart. The ornaments used to display these menus became as fanciful as the cuisine they announced. Sometimes combining the functions of a place name card and souvenir, they always served as the palimpsest of three centuries of culinary history.

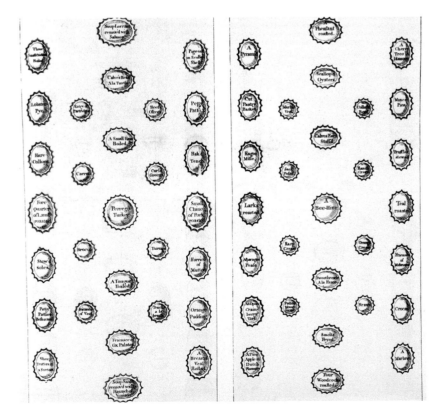

The complicated geometry of French service seems inexplicable to us today, but in the period, almost every book on cookery both in England and the continent advised aspiring hostesses on the elaborate placement of dishes on the table.

resources

A la Vieille Russie Inc.
.781 Fifth Avenue
New York NY 10022
212/752-1727

Animal Art Antiques
1139 Arabella
New Orleans LA 70115
504/895-0518

Au Vieux Paris Antiques
1040 Henri Penne Road
Breaux Bridge LA 70517
337/332-2852

Didier Inc.
3439 Magazine Street
New Orleans LA 70115
504/899-7749

James Robinson
480 Park Avenue
New York NY 10022
212/752-6166

Kenneth W. Rendell Gallery
989 Madison Avenue
New York NY 10021
781/431-1776

Lucullus
610 Chartres St.
New Orleans LA 70130
504/528-9620

M. S. Rau
630 Royal Street
New Orleans LA 70176
800/544-9440

N. P. Trent Antiques
3729 South Dixie Highway
West Palm Beach FL 33405
561/832-0919

S. J. Shrubsale
104 East 57th Street
New York NY 10022
212/753-8920

S. Trowbridge & Co.
213 E. Marcy Street
Santa Fe NM 87509
505/955-8535

Things Finer
100 East San Francisco Street
Santa Fe NM 87501
505/883-5552

Waldhorn and Adler
343 Royal Street
New Orleans LA 70130
504/581-6379

Wirthmore Antiques
3727 Magazine Street
New Orleans LA 70115
504/269-0660

Museums

Gallier House
1118-1132 Royal Street
New Orleans LA 70116
504/523-6722

Herman-Grima House
820 St. Louis Street
New Orleans LA 70112
504/525-5661

Longue Vue House and Gardens
7 Bamboo Road
New Orleans LA 70124
504/488-5488

New Orleans Museum of Art
1 Collins Diboll Circle
New Orleans LA 70124
504/488-2631

page 6: *The Compleat Housewife* by Eliza Smith. Reprinted by permission of the Winterthur Library Printed Book and Periodical Collection.

page 7: *The Useful and the Beautiful.* Reprinted by permission of the Winterthur Library Printed Book and Periodical Collection.

page 98: "The Luncheon of Oysters" by Jean-François de Troy, 1735. Oil on canvas. Photograph by Harry Brejat. Copyright © Réunion des Musées Nationaux / Art Resource, NY, Musée Condé, Chantilly, France.

page 124: "Girls Playing Cards, Storyville," ca. 1911–1913 by E. J. Bellocq. Reprinted by permission of the New Orleans Museum of Art (museum purchase).

page 142: "Scene from the Life of Saint Benedict: A Priest Brings Food to the Saint" (detail) by Giovanni Sodoma, 1508. Copyright © Scala / Art Resource, NY, Abbey, Monte Oliveto Maggiore, Italy.

page 175: Illustration of French service, from "The Complete Housekeeper" by Mary Smith. Rare Books Division, The New York Public Library, Astor, Lenox and Tilden Foundations.

index